The
Hidden Power
of
Social Networks

The

Hidden Power

of

Social Networks

Understanding How
Work Really Gets Done
in Organizations

Rob Cross
Andrew Parker

HARVARD BUSINESS SCHOOL PRESS
Boston, Massachusetts

Two examples in chapter 2 are based on R. Cross, S. P. Borgatti, and A. Parker, "Making Invisible Work Visible: Using Social Network Analysis to Support Strategic Collaboration," *California Management Review* 44, no. 2 (2002): 25–46. Copyright © 2002, with permission of The Regents of the University of California.

Portions of chapter 3 are based on R. Cross, A. Parker, L. Prusak, and S. P. Borgatti, "Knowing What We Know: Supporting Knowledge Creation and Sharing in Social Networks," *Organizational Dynamics* 30, no. 2 (2001): 100–120. Copyright © 2001, with permission from Elsevier Science.

Chapter 4 is based on R. Cross, W. Baker, and A. Parker, "What Creates Energy in Organizations?" *MIT Sloan Management Review* 44, no. 4 (2003): 51–56, by permission of publisher. Copyright © 2003 by Massachusetts Institute of Technology. All rights reserved.

Portions of chapter 5 are based on R. Cross and L. Prusak, "The People Who Make Organizations Go—or Stop," *Harvard Business Review* 80, no. 6 (2002): 1–22.

Portions of chapter 6 are based on Lisa Abrams, Rob Cross, Eric Lesser, and Daniel Levin, "Nurturing Interpersonal Trust in Knowledge-Intensive Work" 17 (4). Copyright © 2003 by Academy of Management Executives. Reprinted by permission of Academy of Management Executives via the Copyright Clearance Center.

978-1-59139-270-5 (ISBN 13)
Library of Congress Cataloging-in-Publication Data
Cross, Robert L., 1967–
    The hidden power of social networks : understanding how work really gets
done in organizations / Rob Cross, Andrew Parker.
        p. cm.
    Includes bibliographical references (p.   ) and index.
    ISBN 1-59139-270-5
    1. Business networks. 2. Employees—Social networks. I. Parker, Andrew,
1966– II. Title.
    HD69.S8C76 2004
    658—dc22

                                                        2003021436

Contents

Preface

PUT AN ORGANIZATIONAL CHART in front of most employees, from line workers to executives, and they will tell you that the boxes and lines do not really capture the way work gets done in their organization. But most will be quick to acknowledge the critical influence that networks of informal relationships have on work and innovation of any importance. As a result of delayering, globalization, and the rise of knowledge-intensive work, social networks—such as those crossing functions in a core process or integrating mergers or alliances—have become a pervasive feature of organizations. These seemingly invisible webs have also become central to performance and execution of strategy. Research shows that appropriate connectivity in well-managed networks within organizations can have a substantial impact on performance, learning, and innovation.[1] Benefits also accrue from well-connected networks between organizations.[2]

Yet despite the importance of networks, executives rarely attempt to assess or support them.[3] Many leaders seem to have been taught in business school, or to have decided from their own experience, that they can't do much about social networks. After all, how can you manage what you can't see? When they do attempt to promote collaboration, many managers assume that network health is a product of information flow and that uniting fragmented networks or developing sparse ones is simply a matter of more and better communication. We can't tell you the number of times we have heard executives claim that team building and an off-site meeting were the keys to improving networks. However, their thinking changes quickly when we ask, "Do you want to attend more meetings and receive more e-mail?" Most executives cringe at the thought and quickly acknowledge that more communication in a world of information overload is not the solution.

Instead, what is desperately needed is a more targeted approach to improving collaboration and network connectivity where they yield the greatest payoff for an organization. Our primary goal in this book is to demonstrate how leaders can accomplish this by tapping into the hidden power of social networks in their organizations.

Of course, concern with social networks and social network analysis is not new. The idea of drawing a picture (called a *sociogram*) of who is connected to whom is often credited to Dr. J. L. Moreno,[4] an early social psychologist. Moreno's first studies in what became the field of sociometry mapped "liking" and "disliking" relationships among five hundred girls in the New York State School for Girls, among two thousand students in a New York public school, and in other communities.[5] Since then, network techniques have influenced a variety of scholarly pursuits. For example, management scholars and sociologists have studied local and virtual communities[6] as well as the relationship between interaction patterns and social phenomena such as power.[7] Cultural anthropologists have applied network analysis to social structure, roles, and kinship systems.[8] Communication researchers have used network analysis to assess the rate of adoption and barriers to diffusion of such things as information, medicine, and the fax machine.[9] And social psychologists have shown how the structure of group communication affects performance.[10]

Only recently, though, has network analysis captured the attention of managers and executives on a broad scale. Malcolm Gladwell's book *The Tipping Point* awakened the general public to the importance of networks. Through rich stories and examples, Gladwell shows how social networks dramatically influence the uptake of ideas and trends in society. Other books, such as *Linked, Six Degrees of Separation*, and *Nexus*, have taken a more technical approach to advancing a science of networks. This work has made broad observations based on patterns found in physical networks, such as the Internet or power grids, or in more contractually oriented networks, such as co-appearances in movies or corporate boards. Yet while aspects of this work translate well to social networks within organizations, managers must also recognize unique features of employee networks.

First, social networks in organizations are dynamic and conditioned by strategy, infrastructure, and the work that is being done at a given time. Often, managerial behavior and organizational design unintentionally and invisibly fragment networks. For example, incentives and work management practices frequently preclude collaboration between colleagues in different departments. Job design can result in some people being sought out for information excessively, thus making them bottlenecks in a network. And staffing practices may lead people with certain expertise to become tightly connected only to those who know the same things. As a result, managers must assess the networks in their organizations with an eye to discovering how organizational context affects network patterns and the achievement of organizational goals.

A second unique feature of employee networks is that information does not flow unchanged through a human network as it does through Internet routers. People add context, interpretation, and meaning as they receive information and pass it along. Remember the game called "telephone"? A simple sentence can become wildly distorted as people whisper it to one another. For example, "The black crow sat on the fence" can quickly become "The red robin flew to its nest." Of course, distortion in employee networks will be greater because most network members aren't necessarily in the same place and focused on the same topic at the same time. And when those in leadership roles or specific network positions have a disproportionate say as to what information is meaningful and which interpretation will carry the day, the distortion can be even worse. As a result, assessing and improving network connectivity in organizations pose different challenges than considering electrons in power grids or information flow through the Internet.

However, managers can use the tools of social network analysis to assess and support important networks within their own organizations, and it's much better to take this targeted approach rather than leave collaboration to chance. Over the past five years, we have been involved with more than sixty strategically important networks in a wide range of well-known organizations. We have worked closely with executives and employees from leading organizations in the fields of consulting, pharmaceuticals, software, electronics and computer manufacturing, consumer products, financial services, petroleum, heavy equipment manufacturing, chemicals, and government to assess and develop strategically important networks. Throughout this research, we had the luxury of returning to most of these organizations at least once to assess the impact of our ideas and refine our thinking as we moved forward. We are aware of no other research on networks in organizations that combines such breadth of involvement across a wide variety of industries with depth of interaction in each organization over time.

In this book, we have synthesized our findings from this and other work to provide a guide for executives and managers to find, assess, and support strategically important networks in their organizations. We hope the pursuit of these ideas is as enjoyable and rewarding for you as it has been for us.

Acknowledgments

THIS BOOK is a product of its topic. All the ideas we share here have been developed in conjunction with a diverse, rich network of colleagues. Collaborations and conversations with various scholars helped to sharpen our thinking methodologically and theoretically. Close work with people in a wide range of organizations continually pushed us to generate practical applications of social network analysis. In short, our own networks allowed us to bridge scholarship and practice, and it is to these myriad relationships that this book is dedicated.

It is impossible in a short acknowledgment to capture the extent to which our thinking has been advanced by the writing of and conversations with network scholars in fields such as communications, management, sociology, and social psychology. Many scholars were both patient and generous with their time in discussions of analytic techniques and the theoretical implications of social networks in organizations. Although this list of people is too long to cover in its entirety, we are very appreciative of conversations and, in some cases, collaborations with Paul Adler, Wayne Baker, Dan Brass, Kathleen Carley, Don Cohen, Noshir Contractor, Jonathon Cummings, Tom Davenport, Nancy Dixon, Gerry Falkowski, Malcolm Gladwell, Tim Hall, Monica Higgins, Herminia Ibarra, Michael Johnson-Cramer, Bill Kahn, David Krackhardt, Valdis Krebs, Daniel Levin, Nitin Nohria, Larry Prusak, Ron Rice, Bill Snyder, Bill Stevenson, Bob Thomas, Dean Walsh, Etienne Wenger, Barry Wellman, and Mike Zack. We are particularly grateful to Steve Borgatti for his guidance on the technical side of social network analysis and his participation with us as a coauthor and consultant to IBM's Knowledge and Organizational Performance Forum.

We are equally indebted to a very large group of people in more than sixty organizations who held our feet to the fire to ensure that our ideas actually worked. These people helped to get us involved with interesting issues inside their organizations and helped us see various applications of network ideas to business concerns. Again, the list of people here is far too lengthy to enumerate, but we are deeply appreciative of the time and effort of many hundreds of people that we have come in contact with in interviews, working sessions, and presentations. In particular, we would like to thank several people we have had the opportunity to work with fairly closely. These include Patti Anklam, Carol Bekar, Derek Binney, Andrew Burton, Larry Chait, Joe Cothrel, Kate Ehrlich, Scott Eliot, David Ewbank, Nathaniel Foote, Kim Glasgow, Doug Gordin, Ryan Gorey, Richard Grainger, Vic Gulas, Giora Hadar, Charlotte Holmlund, Sam Israelit, Al Jacobsen, Andreas Kahnert, Harsh Karandikar, Mary Lee Kennedy, John Kloss, Monique Lambert, Bruno Laporte, Frank Leistner, Richard Livesley, Elaine Lowe, Malia Lowe, Karen Lyons, Diana Martinez-Boyd, Dara Menashi, Terry Naini, Ann Noles, Vivek Parachur, Josh Plaskoff, Jim Poage, Philip Ramsell, Daniel Ranta, Melissie Rumizen, Doug Rush, Lesley Shneier, Tom Short, Matthew Simpson, Ruthanne Smith, Scott Smith, Bill Spencer, Joerg Staeheli, Karen Ughetta, Guillermo Velasquez, Kevin Walker, Leigh Weiss, and Don White. These and many other people have been central to the development of this work.

We also owe a debt of gratitude for the institutional support this work has received. IBM's Knowledge and Organizational Performance Forum provided a fruitful environment in which we were able to develop this work over time. We were very lucky to have a series of helpful and encouraging colleagues in this group: Lisa Abrams, Mike Fontaine, Joe Horvath, Eric Lesser, Eric Mosbrooker, David Millen, David Mundel, Sal Parise, Lisa Sasson, and Dave Snowden. In particular, we want to thank Judith Quillard, who took on the job of editing a lot of our early work. She constantly pushed us to make our work and thinking better and has remained an unwavering supporter. In addition, we are grateful to Accenture's Institute for Strategic Change for its support in developing some of these ideas. We especially thank Sue Cantrell, Tom Davenport, and Bob Thomas for thoughtful collaborations. Finally, we thank the Batten Institute at The Darden Graduate School of Business for underwriting editorial assistance. In particular, we are grateful to Elizabeth O'Halloran for inspiring conversations and support of this work.

On the editorial front, we are extremely grateful to two people who helped bring this work to fruition. First, Melinda Merino carefully guided us through the process with HBS Press. She has provided invaluable guidance on this book, from the original framing of the work to detailed editorial suggestions. Second, this book has been substantially improved by the careful and tireless editing of Amy Halliday. We are truly appreciative of Amy's contributions to this book in terms of both substance and style. We could not have done this without her!

Finally, we owe a tremendous debt of gratitude to our wives. To Debbie, who often scooped up Rachel and Connor outside the office door and patiently endured trips, conference calls, and hours of writing: Your belief in and continual support of me and these ideas are the only reason anything made it to paper. Thank you—Rob.

To Lisa, your patience and encouragement throughout the many hours spent researching and writing this book has made it possible. Thank you—Andrew.

PART ONE

How Work Really Gets Done in Organizations

1

The Hidden Power of Social Networks

It has taken us years, and I think we are still not sure if we are getting things right even after substantial reengineering projects, a move to teams, new HR practices, two acquisitions, and a ton invested in technology. By now we should have reduced costs and created a more nimble company without a focus on hierarchy or fiefdoms. But it's tough to ensure that this is really happening. Most of us in this room have thousands of people we are accountable for stretched across the globe. It's impossible to manage or even know what's going on in the depths of the organization. I mean, each of us can fool ourselves into thinking we're smart and running a tight ship. But really the best we can do is create a context and hope that things emerge in a positive way, and this is tough because you can't really see the impact your decisions have on people. So you just kind of hope what you want to happen is happening and then sound confident when telling others.

—Executive vice president, commercial lending

THIS EXECUTIVE'S frustration likely resonates with your own experience. Whether as a manager presiding over a department or as a member embedded within one, we are all dramatically affected by information flow and webs of relationships within social networks. These networks often are not depicted on any formal chart, but they are intricately intertwined with an organization's performance, the way it develops and executes strategy, and its ability to innovate. For most of us, networks also have a great deal to do with our personal productivity, learning, and career success.

Yet it's not always easy to know what is going on in these large, distributed, and seemingly invisible groups. Reflect for a moment on the network of relationships among the people you work with. You can probably describe your close relationships accurately, but studies show that as you move beyond your immediate circle, your accuracy likely begins to fall off.[1] Given the importance of networks, this lack of understanding can have substantial implications for individual and organizational performance.

The frustrated banker quoted earlier realizes all too keenly that the work of a senior manager is largely about orchestrating the work of others. So central and essential is this role that an entire industry—maybe even several—has emerged, with the goal of revolutionizing the way people get their work done. Over the past two decades, waves of initiatives—such as de-layering, reengineering, total quality management (TQM), teams, supply chain integration, alliances, and implementation of myriad technologies—have washed through the corporate landscape, with varying degrees of success. These efforts to improve efficiency and eradicate bureaucracy have indeed transformed how work gets done. Employees are less constrained than before by formal reporting relationships or overly bureaucratic processes and procedures; important work in most organizations now gets done through networks of employees.

Because work, and the coordination of work, is increasingly negotiated in employee networks, new managerial challenges have emerged. Conventional wisdom suggests that you can't really manage these emergent groups, so executives often do little to support strategically important networks in their organizations. Managers may tout external networks established through alliances and strategic partnerships, and they are sure to acknowledge the importance of internal employee networks. But aside from developing a community of practice or implementing a collaborative technology, most of them don't take any concrete actions to support these networks.[2] This oversight can be costly.

Consider a small network of executives in the exploration and production division of a large petroleum organization. This division was in the midst of implementing a distributed technology to help transfer best practices across drilling initiatives, and the managers were also interested in assessing the ability of the division to create and share knowledge. To help with these efforts, we were asked to conduct a social network analysis of frequent information exchange among the division's top executives. As you can see in figure 1-1, this analysis revealed a striking contrast between the group's formal and informal structures.

FIGURE 1-1a

Formal Versus Informal Structure

FORMAL ORGANIZATIONAL CHART

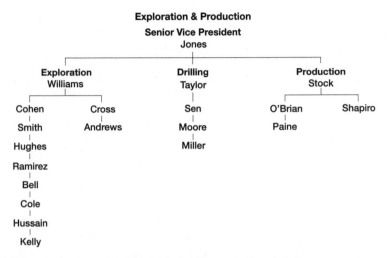

Exploration & Production
Senior Vice President
Jones

Note: This example has been substantially disguised at the request of the organization.

Source: Figures 1-1a and b from R. Cross et al., "Knowing What We Know: Supporting Knowledge Creation and Sharing in Social Networks," *Organizational Dynamics* 30, no. 2 (2001): 100–120. © 2001, reprinted with permission from Elsevier Science.

FIGURE 1-1b

Informal Structure as Revealed by Social Network Analysis

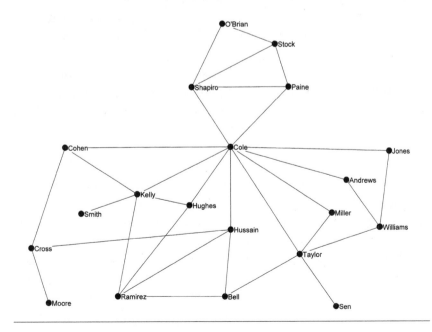

In addition to some political issues that impeded connectivity, three important points about this group's ability to leverage its expertise quickly emerged. First, as is often the case, the network analysis identified midlevel managers critical for information flow whom leaders had not anticipated would be so important. A particular surprise came from the crucial role played by Cole in overall information flow both within the group and between members of the production division and the rest of the network. Cole's reputation for expertise and responsiveness had resulted in his becoming a critical source of all kinds of information. However, the number of requests he received and projects he was involved in had become excessive, not only causing him stress but also often slowing the entire group. Through no fault of his own, Cole had become a bottleneck.

The social network analysis also revealed the extent to which the entire network was disproportionately reliant on Cole. If he were hired away, the company would lose both his knowledge and the relationships he had established, and in many ways these relationships were holding the network together. People would have to scramble to establish informational relationships, and the group's performance would suffer. As a result of the analysis, the organization decided to categorize the requests that Cole received and then allocate some of these domains to other executives. This simple solution unburdened Cole and made the overall network more responsive and robust.

Just as important, the social network analysis helped identify peripheral people who represented untapped expertise. In particular, many of the senior people had become too removed from the group's day-to-day operations. This is common. As people move higher within an organization, their work begins to entail more administrative tasks, making them both less accessible and less knowledgeable about the work of their subordinates. For example, figure 1-1b reveals that the most senior person (Jones) was one of the most peripheral, and his lack of responsiveness often held back the entire network when important decisions needed to be made. The social network diagram helped turn what could have been a difficult confrontation with this executive into a constructive discussion, which led him to commit more of his time to the group.

The analysis also demonstrated the extent to which the production division (the subgroup at the top of the diagram) had become separated from the overall network. Several months before the analysis, this division had been moved to a different floor. After reviewing the network diagram, the executives realized that this physical separation had resulted in fewer serendipitous hallway meetings. Because this lack of communication had driven a series of recent operational problems, they decided to introduce more structured meetings to compensate for this loss.

The Power of a Social Network Perspective

The results of this organization's social network analysis are fairly typical. Even in small, contained groups, executives are often surprised by patterns of collaboration that are quite different from their beliefs and from the formal organization chart. Getting an accurate view of a network helps with managerial decision making and informs targeted efforts to promote effective collaboration. Rather than leave the inner workings of a network to chance, executives can leverage the insights of a social network analysis to address critical disconnects or rigidities in networks and create a sense-and-respond capability deep within the organization.

This is not a trivial issue. Most executives will tell you that effective collaboration is critical to their organization's strategic success. Most, in candid moments, will also admit that they have invested a great deal of time and money to promote collaboration, with few or no results. Often, managers undertake such initiatives without understanding the inner workings of a network, relying on an implicit philosophy that more communication and collaboration are better. For example, managers may implement collaborative technologies with the vague notion that they will help employees interact more seamlessly and that this will improve the quality of their work. They may plan culture change programs, such as efforts in the 1990s to create learning organizations, with the hope that promoting open and honest dialog will improve innovation and performance. Or they may establish communities of practice, as many organizations today are doing, with the intent of promoting knowledge creation and sharing as well as improving the quality and efficiency of work.

Sometimes these initiatives have the desired effect, but the results are not always positive. Organizations can get bogged down. Decision makers can become so consumed that most of their employees cannot get to them in time to seize opportunities. And individual employees get overloaded with e-mail, meetings, and requests for help to a point where their own work, job satisfaction, and even health are damaged.

We can't afford to continue along this path. Rather than pursue initiatives that create connections indiscriminately, managers need to take a more targeted approach, keeping in mind that collaboration has a cost.[3] The power of a network perspective, whether applied to a group or an individual, lies with the precision this view offers.

Managers who target strategic points in social networks can quickly increase an organization's effectiveness, efficiency, and opportunities for innovation. We are not simply suggesting that more connectivity is always better. In networks of any size, it is not possible for everyone to be connected to everyone else, nor is it desirable. An indiscriminate increase in connections can be a drag on productivity. A crucial benefit of network analysis often comes from discovering excessive relation-

TABLE 1-1

Common Social Network Analysis Applications

Supporting partnerships and alliances	Executives are increasingly employing cross-organizational initiatives such as alliances or other forms of strategic partnerships to leverage their organizations' unique capabilities. Social network analysis can illuminate the effectiveness of such initiatives in terms of information flow, knowledge transfer, and decision making.
Assessing strategy execution	Core competencies or capabilities in knowledge-intensive work are usually a product of collaboration across functional or divisional boundaries. Social network analysis allows executives to determine whether the appropriate cross-functional or departmental collaborations are occurring to support strategic objectives.
Improving strategic decision making in top leadership networks	A core function of top executive teams is to acquire information, make sound decisions, and convey those decisions effectively to the broader organization. Social network analysis, when done with both the top leadership team and the next layer down, can provide valuable diagnostic information to leadership. Not only can it help assess connections within a top leadership team, but it can also reveal how information is entering and leaving this group.
Integrating networks across core processes	Informal networks across core processes are often fragmented by functional boundaries. Both cognitive and organizational barriers often keep groups from effectively integrating unique expertise, which can damage quality, efficiency, and innovation. As the process map did for reengineering, social network analysis provides a diagnostic assessment of information and knowledge flow both within and across functions critical to a core process.

ships. This discovery can help managers develop ways to alleviate over-burdened people and decrease time-consuming connections.

In this light, network analysis can be very helpful in revealing patterns of connectivity in specific functions, divisions, or business units. Many groups found on an organizational chart can benefit substantially when viewed through a network lens. These groups include certain departments in a core business process, distributed practices in professional services, and critical support functions such as research and development. More often than not, however, important networks in organizations don't exist on the formal chart and are certainly not on most executives' radar screens, as shown in table 1-1. Groups of people—such as those coming together in a post-merger scenario, alliances, new-product development initiatives, and leadership networks integrating a conglomerate or core business process—need to collaborate well for strategic purposes. Unfortunately, these networks

Promoting innovation	Most innovation of importance is a collaborative endeavor. Whether concerned with new-product development or process improvement initiatives, social network analysis can be particularly insightful in assessing both how a team is integrating its expertise and the effectiveness with which it is drawing on the expertise of others within the organization.
Ensuring integration post-merger or large-scale change	Particularly in knowledge-intensive settings, large-scale change is fundamentally an issue of network integration. Social network analysis, done before a change initiative, can help inform the change process as well as identify central people within the network whom a sponsor might want to engage in design because of their ability to convey information to others. Social network analysis can also be done as a follow-up six to nine months after implementation. Quite often these assessments reveal significant issues that leaders need to address for the initiative to be successful.
Developing communities of practice	Communities of practice are usually not formally recognized within an organization but can be critical to an organization's ability to leverage expertise distributed by virtue of physical location or organizational design. Social network analysis can be used to uncover the key members of the community as well as assess overall health in terms of connectivity.

are often starved of resources and unwittingly fragmented by organizational design and leadership. Network analysis can help ensure that such groups are collaborating appropriately and are not fragmented by physical, functional, hierarchical, or organizational boundaries.

Social Networks and Organizational Performance

Even though networks are pervasive in organizations, it can be hard to get busy executives to pay attention to these seemingly invisible structures. The spoken or unspoken question we often hear is: Why networks now? In the face of operational reports, financial statements, and sales and market share figures (to name only a few of the bits of information vying for attention), why should overextended managers and executives add informal networks to their list of concerns?

We offer two answers to these harried executives. First, as we have described, there is tremendous diagnostic value in understanding how work is or is not getting done deep within an organization. Second, when we look at the sixty organizations we have worked with, we see consistent evidence that well-managed network connectivity is critical to performance, learning, and innovation.

Consider two strategy consulting firms, each claiming to pursue a strategy of customer intimacy. The first had a track record of long relationships with key clients. It often brought in experts to apply fresh knowledge and skills to clients' issues and so maintained consulting relationships for years. In contrast, the second firm, pursuing the same strategy and often the same clients, had less success maintaining relationships with key accounts. In this organization's network analysis, we found that tightly knit subgroups had formed around industry or service offerings. Each group was very good at solving specific problems for clients, but the lack of integration across the groups made it difficult for the firm to present clients with new perspectives. While pursuing the same strategy, the first firm had cultivated better connectivity across industry and service lines by means of staffing practices, human resource policies, leadership, and technology. These efforts made it much more responsive to and successful with clients.

Well-managed connectivity also matters in both temporary and permanent teams.[4] Working with Jonathon Cummings of MIT, we assessed the network patterns and performance of 182 temporary teams engaged in new-product development or process improvement. We found that teams whose networks kept teammates from connecting with each other—such as teams focused on a boss or ones that had split into small subgroups—were significantly worse performers than those in which teammates could leverage one another's expertise more seamlessly.[5]

Employees' personal networks can also provide an important lever for improving performance. In a separate phase of research with Accenture's Institute for Strategic Change, we worked with four organizations (in petrochemicals, pharmaceuticals, electronics, and consulting) to determine the characteristics of high performers in terms of individual expertise, technology use, and networks both inside and outside an organization.[6] We learned that technology use and individual expertise did not distinguish people as high performers. To be sure, not having sufficient expertise or not using technology in the right way could land a person in the bottom 20 percent of performers. However, what distinguished high performers were larger and more diversified personal networks than those of average or low performers. This is consistent with other research findings, in which more diversified networks are associated with early promotion, career mobility, and managerial effectiveness.[7] We will return to this theme in chapter 5.

Our research also underscored the importance of social networks for learning and innovation in organizations. When we think of where people turn for information or knowledge, we usually think of databases, the Internet, or more traditional repositories, such as file cabinets or policy and procedure manuals. Yet even though databases (and the staff to support them) have grown to mammoth proportions, they are often underused because employees are more likely to turn to colleagues for information.[8] In summarizing a decade's worth of studies, Tom Allen of MIT indicated that engineers and scientists were roughly five times as likely to turn to a person for information as to an impersonal source such as a database or a file cabinet. In other settings, research has consistently shown that whom you know has a significant impact on what you come to know, because relationships are critical for obtaining information, solving problems, and learning how to do your work.[9]

On reflection this is not very surprising, but in our work we wanted to reconfirm this point given the recent explosion of information and technology. Each time we conducted a network assessment, we also surveyed employees about their use of available technologies. Only once did we find an organization where employees rated internal databases or knowledge management systems as more effective than the Internet in helping them complete their work. In *no* cases did we see any technology come close to the importance people gave to other people for finding information and learning how to get work done. This is not to suggest that organizations should get rid of their databases; they constitute rich sources of memory that workers often leverage after consulting a personal network for help in locating a document or bit of information.[10] However, some portion of the millions of dollars most organizations are investing in underutilized technologies can be effectively reallocated to initiatives that promote vibrant employee networks.

Part One of this book describes how work really gets done in organizations through these informal networks of people and provides managers a means of assessing employee networks. This chapter has provided a brief overview of how social network analysis can shed light on problems of collaboration and connectivity in organizations and can provide managers a more effective and strategic way to address these problems. Chapters 2 and 3 demonstrate specific methods for viewing collaboration, in terms of both active information flow and relational dimensions that affect the quality and likelihood of collaboration. Chapter 4 shows how energy in networks impacts work and offers a new way for managers to think about how collaboration, innovation, and learning are occurring—or not occurring—in their organizations.

Throughout these chapters, we do not present the most sophisticated network analysis techniques. Instead, we describe the ones managers have consistently found useful. Network analysis is complex, with one of the leading primers running more than eight hundred pages long,[11] and one of the most widely used software programs housing literally hundreds of routines to choose from.[12] At one time or another, we have placed almost all of these analyses in front of managers to determine which ones consistently yielded actionable insights. Clearly, more sophisticated analyses can be helpful in scholarship, the physical sciences, and more stable social settings than a typical network of employees. More often than not, though, managers find the basic analyses we describe here more than sufficient.

In addition to analyzing social networks, our research uncovered a host of actions—beyond simply communicating more and implementing a technology—that can promote vibrant employee networks. Part Two of this book sets forth practical ways for managers to promote healthy networks after they have identified opportunities for improvement. Chapter 5 describes ways for managers and executives to improve networks by looking at individual employees and their positions within a network as well as by promoting more effective personal networks, including their own. Chapter 6 describes how to promote connectivity based on a network's overall stage of development. Chapter 7 reviews critical elements of organizational context (structure, technology, HR practices, cultural values, and leaders' behavior) that must support new patterns of collaboration to keep a network from reverting to dysfunctional configurations. Chapter 8 takes a look at future trends in networks as well as the potential drawbacks of an excessive focus on networks and misuse of network analysis.

Finally, for those interested in additional practical tools, appendix A provides a step-by-step guide for conducting a social network analysis, and appendix B presents exercises for promoting and sustaining healthy networks in organizations. Additionally, the Web site (www.robcross.org) contains diagnostic material and software that enhances the book and the practical use of these ideas in organizations.

Making Invisible Work Visible

In today's flatter organizations, work of significance demands effective collaboration within and across functional, physical, and hierarchical boundaries. Now more than ever this work occurs through informal networks of people, providing managers a distinct challenge. Through our research and experience working with executives on building and improving networks in their organizations, we have found that executives can do a lot to support important employee networks. And we have seen that those who make an effort to improve the connectivity of such groups are likely to be rewarded with a more effective and innovative organization. In chapter 2 we describe one of the ways that managers can improve collaboration and communication across boundaries by using network analysis to find and fix critical disconnects in organizations.

Note: Throughout the book, you will see a variety of network diagrams. Some, like the one in figure 1-1, are simple. Others are more complex. Figure 1-2 presents a brief primer to help you become familiar with how to read these diagrams.

FIGURE 1-2

How to Read a Network Diagram

Lines and Arrows. The diagram shows the flow of information within a new-product development team. Each line indicates an information link between two people; arrows represent the direction of the relationship (incoming arrows show that the person is a source of information; outgoing arrows show that the team member seeks information from the linked party).

Central People. Network diagrams make clear who the most prominent people within a group are. On this team, nine people rely on Paul for information. His colleagues in finance come to him, but so do people in marketing and manufacturing. Paul himself does not reach out to people outside finance. The diagram alone can't tell us whether Paul's impact is positive or negative. If the group is overly dependent on him, he may be a bottleneck, slowing the flow of information and holding up decisions. On the other hand, people like Paul often play a very positive role, providing valuable information and holding a group together.

Peripheral People. Some people are only loosely connected to a network; a few may be completely isolated—members in theory but not in practice. In this network, no one goes to Carl for information, and Kevin is out of the loop entirely. As is true with central people, the diagram alone doesn't say anything about the value of peripheral people. Such outsiders often turn out to be underutilized resources, and integrating them can be critical to a network's effectiveness and efficiency. However, sometimes people are peripheral for good reason; perhaps they are trying to manage work-family balance or are specialists such as research scientists, who need to maintain strong ties to academia. And on occasion they are out there because they lack skills, social and otherwise, for the job.

Subgroups. Groups within a network often arise as a product of location, function, hierarchy, tenure, age, or gender. In this case, the team is split by function; very little information is being shared between the three groups. Moreover, connections in marketing and finance are sparse, whereas the manufacturing subgroup is tightly knit. That can be good or bad. It may be that the manufacturing people have developed communication practices that the team as a whole could use to its benefit. It's also possible that those people rely on one another so heavily that they are preventing integration. Only follow-up interviews can reveal which scenario is true.

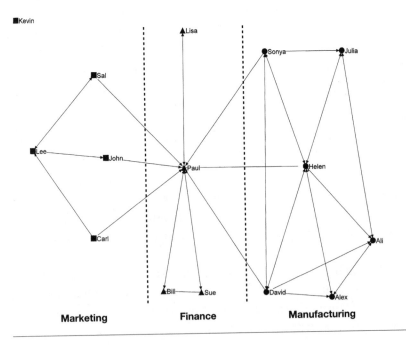

Marketing   Finance   Manufacturing

2

Across the Great Divide

Finding and Fixing Critical Disconnects in Organizations

The network analysis helped me quickly get a sense of what I had stepped into. I am an old hand at the work, but being new to the organization and the people I was supposed to be managing, it would have taken me at least six months to make the rounds to get a sense of what was going on. Even then, I would still only get some people's perspectives and opinions and have things wrong by other accounts. I didn't have too much time to try and figure this out because I was supposed to be making things happen immediately, not six months later. The network analysis taught me a lot about the inner workings of this group, and most importantly showed me some splits in the network that we really had to address quickly.

—Director of R&D of a global
manufacturing organization

AS THIS SENIOR EXECUTIVE recounts, network analysis can help incoming leaders quickly assess and improve employee networks. Mergers, internal restructurings, and turnover often thrust managers into leadership positions. These new leaders usually have little time to build diverse, and perhaps far-flung, employees into groups that can collaborate fluidly on complex projects. Yet their careers and the success of their organizations often hinge on ensuring that employees are collaborating effectively. This executive had been asked to take charge

15

of a recently formed research function. Nine months earlier, senior management had become concerned with the organization's ability to develop and disseminate leading-edge manufacturing processes and technologies. As a result, a research function had been formed from highly skilled subject-matter experts drawn from across the organization. In the old structure, these experts were dispersed in myriad functions and business units. In the new, they were brought under one leader to ensure focus and consistency in manufacturing processes and technologies.

A network analysis of this group gave the incoming executive a great deal of insight. For example, he was surprised by the central role some employees were playing and was concerned with the extent to which some of the leading experts were peripheral members of the group. And although he was pleased to learn of practices in some countries that promoted effective collaboration, he was concerned with clustering in the network, which indicated that the division was not yet well integrated. The new division's success relied on collaboration and cross-fertilization of ideas among employees on the front line. However, as figure 2-1 reveals, most employees were still collaborating only with others in their own country. In fact, the only connections across countries were those of the leadership team along with a few relationships formed during past projects.

Many managers attempt to bridge physical distance by using collaborative technologies, such as virtual problem-solving spaces and on-line resumes that help employees find colleagues with specific expertise. This organization had adopted these technologies but found that people still relied on those they knew and trusted, and not a database of self-proclaimed experts, for advice on whom to seek out. So one goal for this executive was to help employees develop an awareness of and trust in their colleagues' expertise throughout the network. The fragmentation of this network was also a result of individual and division-level incentives that were part of the prior organizational structure but still were keeping employees focused on work within their own country. Another part of the problem was cultural. People in different countries preferred to interact with others of the same nationality. And, as often occurs in technical work, a "not-invented-here" mentality contributed substantially to the isolation of subgroups.

After an off-site meeting, the division's leaders took several actions. First, they held a meeting of all employees. But instead of a couple of presentations followed by a cocktail hour (where people will always

FIGURE 2-1

Information Flow in a Distributed R&D Group

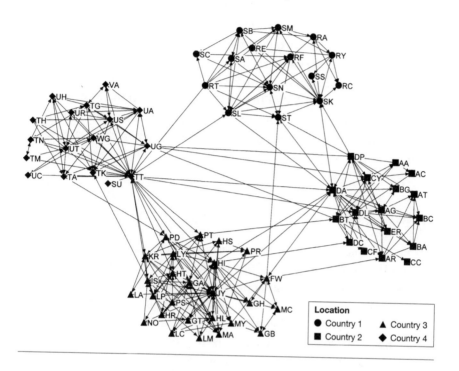

cluster with those they already know), the meeting consisted of a series of workshops focused on projects under way in various countries. In these joint problem-solving sessions, people not only found solutions and shared recent successes but also learned about one another's expertise. And to make sure that this was not a one-time event, the managers arranged monthly conference calls where people followed up on the projects discussed during the workshops. The face-to-face meeting was critical for initiating relationships. These ties were then maintained and strengthened through virtual means such as conference calls, Web casts, and other collaborative tools.

Just as important, the firm's leaders began to adopt policies and procedures that encouraged collaboration throughout the network. First, in hiring they began to target collaborative behaviors in interviews rather than focus heavily on individual accomplishment. The only part of the network that had been screening for collaborative ability was, as you might expect, the best-connected subgroup. Second, the managers changed project management and evaluation practices to ensure that people reached out to colleagues for advice at the start of a research program. This behavior was taken very seriously in project evaluations and encouraged ties across country lines as well as helped overcome the not-invented-here mentality. Third, the leaders centralized staffing rather than staffing locally from each country. The goal here was to facilitate cross-group collaboration and to ensure that the best expertise was placed on each research project. Finally, they redesigned individual performance metrics to focus less on individual productivity and more on collaborative behaviors.

Revealing Disconnects

In this example, network analysis uncovered critical disconnects that were undermining the work of this group, and helped the incoming executive develop a targeted and efficient plan to address them. Revealing such disconnects is one of the most powerful results of a network analysis. Sophisticated analytical techniques can be used to help identify subgroups based strictly on network patterns.[1] In addition, it is always important to look for clustering based on characteristics of people in the network or the organization's formal structure. In doing this, we first define what a network should look like if it is functioning well and then look for clustering that might keep the group from getting its work done.

We always look for clustering by virtue of the following:

- Relative tenure in an organization: Do mentoring relationships exist? Are new people integrated effectively?

- Gender, age, ethnicity, or education: Do social characteristics fragment groups?

- Project staffing: Is cross-fertilization of ideas occurring across key initiatives?

- Employee status: Are we learning from key contractors and creating a context where temporary employees can succeed?

- Task interdependence: Are roles and processes streamlined, or do they overload people or entire networks?

We also consider four aspects of organizational structure that almost always divide networks at points that affect organizational performance. First, as described earlier, physical distance is important because distances of even a few feet between offices can decrease the likelihood of collaboration. In addition, we look for fragmentation across functional or departmental boundaries, hierarchical levels, and organizational lines (as in alliances or mergers).

Cross-Functional Collaboration in a Leadership Team

Let's look at another example: the professional services division of a global technology organization. Senior management was relying on two points of integration in this rapidly expanding division. First, each practice area needed to be integrated with target customer accounts so that the entire division could bring its best expertise to these multimillion-dollar accounts. For example, the infrastructure practice, which designed and implemented technical infrastructure solutions, needed to apply work and knowledge from one customer to the next.

Second, each of the practices needed to collaborate with the sales and marketing groups so that solutions could be cross-sold. For example, a business consulting engagement could lead to an outsourcing arrangement or to a large infrastructure implementation. But these important sales would happen only if managers from different groups were collaborating in the sale and delivery of services.

The division had grown rapidly and had succeeded in accelerating the technology organization's introduction of high-value services. However, after a year and a half of frenetic growth, the top executives of the consulting division had become concerned that their organization was not working the way they had hoped. Many of them believed there was minimal collaboration among people with important kinds of expertise, resulting in missed sales opportunities and, on occasion, low-quality work. The organization undertook a network analysis to help illustrate where collaboration was and was not occurring. The analysis included members of the executive team and the people who reported directly to them. The executives were responsible for ensuring that all sales opportunities included substantial service components. Their direct reports managed the resources and clients: These were the people who sold and delivered solutions to customers. Thus, collaboration across practice areas and across hierarchical levels was critical to the effective functioning of the division as a whole.

Figure 2-2a shows information flow in this extended leadership team. Each practice is coded in a different shape, with large shapes representing the top executives and smaller shapes their direct reports. Figure 2-2b shows the same network with the top executives removed. By pulling out the top nine executives and mapping the flow of information among them, we assessed the extent to which this group was effectively collaborating as a decision-making body. Furthermore, by considering the top management team in the context of the larger network of fifty-four people, we were able to see how they tapped into the larger leadership network for informational purposes and communicated decisions back to this group. Given the strategic importance of their decisions, understanding sources of information could provide critical insight into ways to improve the effectiveness of the top management team and correct biases in an executive's personal network.

FIGURE 2-2a

Network of Top Fifty-Four Executives

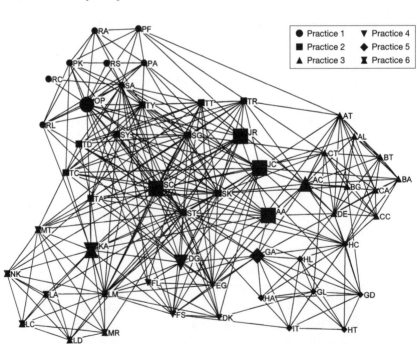

In terms of cross-functional connections, figure 2-2b shows that what looks like a well-connected network becomes fragmented in the absence of leadership collaboration. In some cases, this kind of network pattern might be appropriate. For example, it is often more important for operating room nurses and physicians to take direction from lead surgeons than to collaborate among themselves. But in most work, an overreliance on leadership can result in lack of responsiveness to key customers and missed business opportunities. In our example, despite good intentions and engaged executive leadership, the equivalent of functional silos had emerged under each of the executives. This was a problem because people lower in the hierarchy needed to connect across divisions to provide competitive solutions for customers.

When we reported these results to the executives, their interest was palpable. The disconnection among people in the individual practices was greater than they had realized, and the diagrams made clear that cross-functional collaboration, which was critical to this organization's

FIGURE 2-2b

Network Fragments Without the Top Nine Executives

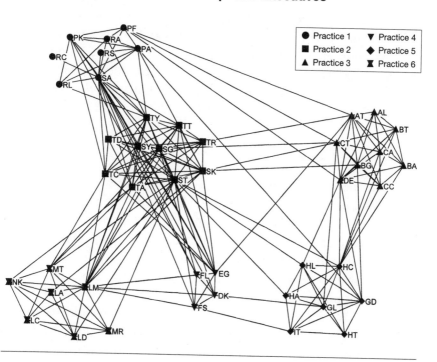

strategy, was haphazard at best. The precision of the network analysis helped the executives to diagnose current problems in business development across the practices. They were also able to predict the areas that would present the greatest future challenges given the organization's business plans.

As a result of the analysis, the executives identified seven problematic junctures and took actions to bridge these gaps. For example, one of the key gaps lay between business consulting and the managed services practice. Business consulting provided an exceptional opportunity to sell services, but collaboration between the two practices was limited to three weak connections. Another important disconnect existed between the enterprise customer group and the business consulting practice. Two weeks after the network analysis, the managers of these two groups agreed to create a position for a senior manager who would work on developing and implementing a sales plan and managing the resulting business opportunities. The business consulting practice itself restructured its operational model to reflect the need to work collaboratively across the practices.

In addition to focusing on the problem points between the practices, all the managers took an active interest in applying the network analysis results to their own groups. Half-day leadership sessions were held for employees in each of the practices to allow them to assess their internal connectivity as well as opportunities for integrating across business lines. These meetings helped managers understand the importance of networks and of creating grass-roots initiatives throughout the practices to promote network connectivity.

Post-Merger Integration

Similarly, network analysis can help promote the success of a single acquisition or a conglomerate formed by a series of acquisitions. For example, we mapped the relationships of a *Fortune* 500 organization's top 126 executives, who were dispersed across eight divisions. The organization had grown by acquisition over several years in the hope that the acquired companies would pool expertise to develop and market new products and services. Given this strategy, the CEO was acutely aware of the need to create a leadership network that would recognize opportunities in one part of the organization and would know enough of what others in the conglomerate knew to combine

TABLE 2-1

Collaboration Across Merged Divisions in a Conglomerate

	Division 1	Division 2	Division 3	Division 4	Division 5	Division 6	Division 7	Division 8
Division 1	33%							
Division 2	5%	76%						
Division 3	11%	18%	45%					
Division 4	2%	11%	21%	38%				
Division 5	6%	7%	12%	6%	75%			
Division 6	7%	2%	13%	7%	2%	76%		
Division 7	1%	3%	16%	6%	8%	2%	36%	
Division 8	10%	2%	9%	6%	3%	10%	0%	90%

resources in response to these opportunities. Because this was not happening, we were invited to conduct a social network analysis of the top two layers of management in this conglomerate.

Although we generated various network diagrams, the most insightful view came from a simple table demonstrating collaborative activity among the top executives. Table 2-1 outlines the percentage of collaborative relationships that existed within and between each division (out of 100 percent possible in each cell). The table revealed opportunities for one division to learn from the practices of another division to improve collaboration. Similarly, we determined which of the merged organizations (termed *divisions* in table 2-1) had integrated well with other divisions. For example, a quick review of table 2-1 shows that divisions 3 and 4 had reasonable levels of collaboration, whereas divisions 1 and 7 did not.

There were various reasons for the limited collaboration we found. In some situations, members of the executive team were not sure what a given division did and so did not know how to involve it in projects. In others, cultural barriers restricted people from seeking information outside their own division. And in still other instances, the product offerings of the acquired companies were not as complementary as executives had expected.

In the organizations we have worked with, this kind of cross-boundary view has been effective in helping managers identify points where collaboration is not occurring and target improvements. Of course, managers seldom want high levels of collaboration among *all* departments in an organization. People have a finite amount of time for developing and maintaining relationships. But with network analysis, executives can define precisely the constellation of relationships that are worth the investment of time and energy. For example, in this conglomerate, division 1 needed to be well connected only to divisions 3, 5, and 6 to help the organization meet its strategic objectives. Rather than engage in a companywide initiative to improve collaboration, the leaders undertook targeted, and ultimately more successful, initiatives at these and other specific junctures.

Collaboration Across the Hierarchy

Hierarchy is another critical boundary that can affect collaboration within organizations. Some networks are similar to reporting relationships, which can constrain information flow and innovation. Others are more fluid and operate with less regard to the formal chain of command. What is good or bad practice depends on the kind of work the organization does. The benefit of network analysis is that it allows a manager to diagnose the extent to which hierarchy conditions information flow.

Just as we analyzed cross-divisional collaboration in the social network of the conglomerate mentioned earlier, we can also assess collaboration across hierarchical levels within any organization. For example, we worked with a strategy consulting practice of an accounting firm. This organization was keenly interested in ensuring that its industry and service expertise were being shared across the practice and that employees could easily acquire information from others. We ran several analyses of this group. One of the more interesting ones concerned the way collaboration within the practice was affected by hierarchy.

Table 2-2 shows connectivity across hierarchical levels. In contrast to the conglomerate example, here we display a full table to show asymmetry in information-seeking relationships. (In other words, a consultant might turn to a partner for information but not vice versa.) This table shows information seeking going from the rows to the columns. For example, 23 percent of possible relationships existed in which part-

TABLE 2-2

Information Flow Across Hierarchical Levels

	Partner	Manager	Senior	Staff
Partner	**67%**	23%	13%	3%
Manager	56%	**46%**	34%	27%
Senior	25%	24%	**21%**	18%
Staff	33%	36%	30%	**21%**

ners reached out to managers for information, whereas 56 percent of possible relationships were directed from managers to partners. Viewing such asymmetrical relationships can help managers pinpoint roles, functions, or physical locations that have become bottlenecks.

Table 2-2 reveals several important points. First, looking down the diagonal, you can quickly see that the partners (and, to a lesser extent, the managers) are fairly well connected. This is common in most organizations. We often see high levels of connectivity among the senior people because they have many opportunities to interact (for example, in planning sessions and budget meetings), and they tend to be part of the same distribution lists and virtual forums.

In contrast, if you continue down the diagonal, you see fewer connections between senior and staff consultants. As is typical in consulting, staff consultants were hired and then shipped out to client sites for long stretches. Because they did not have many ways to connect with their home organization, they had a hard time getting information and learning organization norms from their peers. Our interviews revealed that the 40 percent turnover rate in the consulting staff was mainly caused by disaffection and feelings of disconnectedness among these people.

To improve the situation the firm made several changes, including extensive orientation efforts that rotated new hires. Leaders adopted a different consulting model that focused on bringing all employees back into the office on Fridays and began to hold monthly meetings for senior and staff consultants. A collaborative space was created, and a small budget was allocated for social events and other innovative means of improving connectivity.

In many organizations we find a comparative lack of connectivity among those lower in the hierarchy. In part this is a function of group size: It is much harder to sustain high levels of connectivity with the larger numbers of people lower in the hierarchy. This is an important managerial issue; however, because the people with the best and most relevant expertise are often on the front lines, it is rare for them to learn about one another's expertise or develop social ties that encourage sharing. Occasionally, lack of connectivity lower in the hierarchy can also mean that too many requests are elevated up the chain of command, quickly turning leaders into bottlenecks.

In this case, we had breakfast with the partners in charge of the consulting practice before conducting an all-employee workshop on the results of the network analysis. At the breakfast we learned that each partner believed hierarchy did not constrain information flow at all; they all felt that people were comfortable seeking them out for information and that they were accessible to all others in the network. As the workshop participants filed into the room, however, the scene became almost comical. Immediately in front of us and to our right was a table where all the partners sat. To our left and a little farther back was a cluster of tables where the managers had congregated. Senior consultants were a little farther away, and the staff consultants, as you probably have guessed, were at the back of the room.

This seating arrangement closely mirrored the network analysis results. If you look across the row of the partners in table 2-2, you see two things: Not only do those higher in the hierarchy cluster among themselves, but they also seek information substantially less often from those progressively lower in the hierarchy. In contrast, considering the entire table, you find a fairly robust tendency for people to reach up in the hierarchy for information. The result, although the partners were unaware of it, was that those higher in the group were significant bottlenecks.

Leaders often have difficulty understanding the effect of hierarchy on a network without some form of systematic feedback, such as a network analysis. For most members of a network, having to work through the levels of a hierarchy results in either slow response or missed opportunities. Yet leaders often don't experience this frustration. They move rapidly from one meeting to the next, making critical decisions at every point. In their day-to-day experience, things happen and decisions are made very quickly. They are seldom aware that peripheral people often wait weeks for a response to an important question or, worse, decide not to bother asking the question.

This is the case in many organizations. However, in our experience, it is much more prevalent in professional services than in other sectors such as manufacturing or government. In many kinds of professional services work, there is often not a single right answer but many plausible ones. Those in power often dictate the correct course of action and can quickly create networks that are overly reliant on them. The prescription in such cases is to identify and reallocate information domains and decision rights to others in the network. But this can be tough if leaders like to be sought out or have begun to believe that they really do always have the best answer.

Collaboration Across Organizational Boundaries

To this point, we have focused on collaboration within an organization. However, it's also crucial for managers to understand how new information and insights cross networks linking one organization to another. In this way, you can uncover substantial learning biases of a group or even an entire organization. Research groups are often highly dependent on ties to academic institutions or technical associations. Professional services firms focus on developing and learning from rich relationships with clients. And top executives often rely on colleagues in other organizations for information on new markets, accounts, or innovative organizational practices. In these and other groups, external relationships are critical to the health of the network. We can miss these relationships if we focus only on internal collaboration.

Let's look at another example, a research and development group in a major pharmaceutical organization. Pharmaceutical R&D units face great pressures to transform ideas into new products, and collaboration not only spurs innovation but also reduces drug development time. It typically takes many years and hundreds of millions of dollars to move a new drug through the pipeline to commercial production, and each day not on the market can mean substantial revenue losses.[2] Because of these costs, this R&D group considered it a strategic imperative to have well-connected social networks and effective collaboration among its research scientists around the world. However, this was a particular challenge for this organization because its twelve R&D facilities were located throughout Asia, North America, and Europe.

Our network analysis focused on two kinds of collaboration among employees: internally between R&D sites and externally with academic scientists. The results revealed opportunities to build relationships across drug development projects as well as research facilities. The number of intersite interactions was low, with one site in complete isolation. By contrast, the number of interactions between company scientists and external academics was quite high. A small number of individuals were responsible for a large percentage of the information-sharing interactions, both internally and externally. It turned out that twelve people in the network were responsible for most of the connectivity with academics. In fact, removal of only the four most-connected people reduced external connectivity by more than half. Clearly, in terms of both internal and external connectivity, this network depended heavily on those scientists and would suffer if they departed.

Too little external connectivity can also be a cause of concern. For example, in the information networks in a well-known software organization and a major strategy-consulting firm, we found very high levels of internal connectivity but extremely low external connectivity. And, unfortunately, the only people with external ties tended to be new hires, who often were not listened to until they had proven themselves within the organization. Of course, by that time they were usually so ingrained in the network that they had quit seeking information via external relationships.

This problem is hardly confined to these two organizations. Again and again, we have seen that leading firms in an industry sector have a marked tendency to become insular. What is worse is that the most insular people in the group often are leaders or highly regarded experts. In other words, the people least likely to be learning from those outside the network are the people on whom the whole network is relying. Unfortunately, they are often too consumed by the demands of the group to reach out to other organizations, associations, or universities, and thus new information, perspectives, and ideas can be missed. The personal network assessments we turn to in chapter 5 are powerful means of improving this potentially significant bias in both group and individual learning.

Alliances and Partnerships

Alliances and other forms of strategic partnerships offer special opportunities for social network analyses. These initiatives are undertaken to promote collaboration and sometimes knowledge transfer between organizations. However, leaders in one organization usually have minimal insight into their counterpart's organization, and collaboration can be heavily conditioned by legal restrictions and cultural and leadership differences, as well as differences in each company's level of expertise. A network analysis can tell executives whether appropriate points of connectivity exist across organizations and whether governance is restricting collaboration.

For example, consider an alliance between two well-known organizations that came together to bring a product to market. One organization held a patent and understood the science behind the product. The other had manufacturing and distribution expertise. It was presumed that the product could be introduced much more effectively and efficiently if the two organizations worked together. Of course this required effective collaboration, which our network assessment showed to be less than desirable at certain key intersections. We did find effective collaboration between the organizations' sales and technical groups. However, minimal connections existed between people in the two marketing groups, who desperately needed to collaborate to attain the alliance's billion-dollar sales goal.

Many reasons for this disconnect emerged. The organizations were located in different cities and were configured differently, and these differences caused problems in aligning the groups based on the alliance agreement. Furthermore, no effort had been made to help employees in each group become aware of their counterparts' expertise in the other organization. Except for channels formed early in a few meetings, additional relationships developed only by serendipity.

Additionally, the organizations had very different cultural norms, a fact that became apparent on two levels. First, the rigid hierarchical nature of one of the organizations precluded spontaneous connection between the two. Second, one organization was very traditional, whereas the other was more progressive. Subtle comments made in meetings between the organizations revealed these different value orientations and seeded an us/them mentality that fragmented the network.

Governance of such partnerships can also often be a problem. Some contractual arrangements are too prescriptive when it comes to interaction and collaboration, and others are not prescriptive enough. In this case, the lead representative from one of the companies turned out to be both the most sought-out person in the network and the person with whom most people wanted to communicate more. This is one example of how governance in an alliance, if underspecified, can be dangerous. When decision rights are not clear to members of a group, people elevate even the most trivial decisions up the hierarchy.

Here, one person held a great deal of decision-making power and by virtue of this had become a bottleneck in the network. She was working long hours just trying to keep up and was loved by the people she worked with because of her hands-on, action-oriented approach. But by virtue of the number of people in the network and the complexity of the issues they coped with, she had become overly central. Network analysis can be a powerful way to help such people reconsider governance in alliances by focusing precisely on decision rights, accountability in projects, and information flow.

Critical Connections

With social network analysis, managers have a means of assessing and supporting groups of employees when effective collaboration is critical to strategic success. Although managers cannot mandate that people develop relationships, they can take a range of actions that increase the likelihood of effective collaboration at important junctures. To this point, we have been concerned only with information flow in organizations. However, there are other dimensions of relationships that promote the quality of collaboration as well as different kinds of information flow that an executive might be concerned with—topics we turn to next.

3

Knowing What We Know

Developing a Sense-and-Respond Organizational Capability

> We definitely need to home in on some of the disconnects you found in the information network. At the same time, I think we need to create a broader ability for employees to get information from others when they need it. This is not so much about pushing more information through a group but about developing relationships that can be rapidly sought out when needed. I can get information from others when I want it because I'm the boss. But we need this kind of responsiveness built deeply into networks binding physicians, nurses, and administrators because the cost of them not getting timely information can be catastrophic.
>
> —*Senior hospital administrator*

THIS SENIOR HOSPITAL ADMINISTRATOR hit on an important truth: Network effectiveness hinges on more than just information flow. When we assess information-seeking networks, we typically get a snapshot of collaboration, a sense of who is connected to whom based on the current set of projects in an organization. In dynamic settings such as professional services, software development, or health care, networks should adapt when new projects demand different kinds of information and expertise. Ideally, as imagined by our health care executive, these networks can *surge:* sense opportunities or problems and rapidly tap into the right expertise for an effective response. You can't accomplish this by pushing information onto employees. Rather, as new challenges and opportunities arise, employees need to know who has relevant expertise—who knows what in the network.

Take, for example, a highly skilled group in a consulting firm that was organized to provide thought leadership and specialized support to the firm's knowledge-management consultants. The group was composed of people who had advanced degrees or extensive industry experience in either strategy and organizational design or technical fields such as data warehousing and architecture. By integrating highly specialized expertise, management hoped to differentiate the firm from competitors that were focusing exclusively on either technical or organizational approaches. When we encountered this group, the founding partner had recently retired. The new partner in charge felt that the team was not leveraging its abilities as effectively as it could and asked us to conduct a network analysis.

As shown in figure 3-1a, the information-seeking network revealed not one group but two distinct subgroups. Ironically, the group had fragmented according to the two skill sets it was supposed to be integrating. The subgroup on the left in figure 3-1a was skilled in the "softer" issues of strategy and organizational design, often focusing on culture and other organizational approaches to improving the creation and sharing of knowledge. The subgroup on the right was composed of people skilled in the "harder" aspects of knowledge management, such as information architecture and databases.

In the senior partners' minds, the group had been given a charter to integrate these unique skill sets, and they thought that incentives, technology, and formal organizational design had changed sufficiently to support this mission. In reality, people gravitated to those who read what they read, went to the conferences they went to, and worked on the projects they worked on. Over time, employees in each subgroup had lost sight of what those in the other subgroup could contribute to a consulting engagement. Thus, even when there were opportunities to incorporate each other's skills to serve clients, neither group knew enough of what the other knew to involve them in projects.

Alam, a manager in the center of the diagram, played an interesting role. Although he was not the most senior person, he appeared to be one of the most important. Lose Alam, and the only relationship bridging the two subgroups would be between the partner in charge of the group and a senior manager who felt he should have been in charge—not a productive relationship. But you can interpret this diagram in two

FIGURE 3-1a

Information Sharing: Before Changes

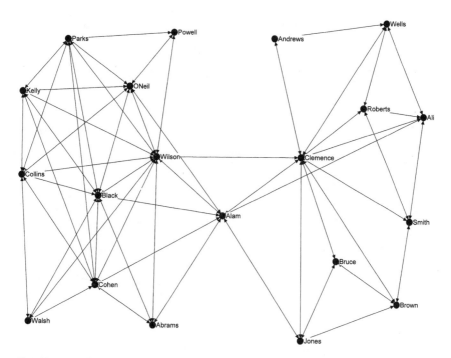

Note: Names are disguised in this example at the request of the organization.

Source: Figures 3-1a and b from R. Cross et al., "Making Invisible Work Visible: Using Social Network Analysis to Support Strategic Collaboration," *California Management Review* 44, no. 2 (2002): 25–46. © 2002, reprinted with permission of The Regents of the University of California.

ways. One is that Alam was critical for holding the group together. A second is that he was a bottleneck and was fragmenting the group.

It turned out that Alam was a bottleneck. Early in his career, he honed his technical skills, graduating with a computer science degree and working in the IT department of a Wall Street bank. Later he developed strategy and organizational expertise by earning an MBA from an Ivy League school and working for one of the premier consultancies. With this experience, Alam was the only person in the network who understood the work and spoke the language of both subgroups. This unique position gave him the opportunity to help people in each subgroup connect.

But this is not what he chose to do. Instead, he spent time telling people in one subgroup not to bother contacting members in the other subgroup because he could do everything they could. Then he told

FIGURE 3-1b

Information Sharing: Nine Months after Changes

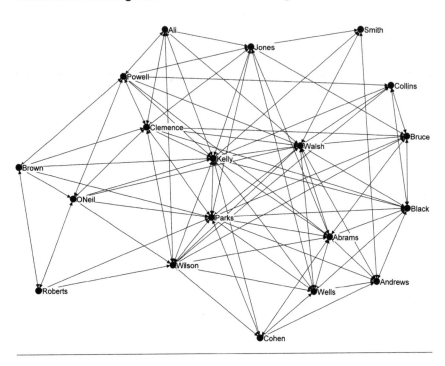

those in the other subgroup the same story. On paper, Alam looked great. He had the highest revenue generation and billable hours of all the managers and was likely to be the next partner. But his tactics for excelling individually ensured that no one in either subgroup developed an awareness of how to collaborate with people in the other subgroup.

In a lengthy facilitated session, the group members assessed and discussed the isolation of the two specialties as well as more pointed concerns about certain members' expertise going untapped while others had become information-sharing bottlenecks. By the time we conducted this session, Alam had transferred to another practice for reasons unrelated to our network analysis. However, it was in this session that we slowly began to see how his prior actions had kept the groups apart.

As a result of the discussion, the group made important operational changes targeted at improving members' awareness of one another's expertise. First, a variety of internal projects—ranging from writing white papers to developing a project-tracking database—were staffed with at least one person from each subgroup. Second, the partner in charge implemented mixed-revenue sales goals so that managers would be motivated to sell projects that included both a technical and an organizational component. Finally, several new communication forums were created, including weekly status calls, e-mail updates, and a project-tracking database. These helped each member keep up-to-date on what others were doing.

The result of these changes was significant. As shown in figure 3-1b, a network analysis conducted nine months later revealed a well-integrated group whose members were sharing information much more effectively. Over the next several months, the group began to sell more work that integrated technical and organizational skills. And, as had originally been envisioned, this integration often differentiated the firm from its competitors.

A Latent Network View

The underlying problem that plagued the specialists in the consulting firm—a lack of awareness of the expertise within the group—is by no means unusual. We have heard many stories where an organization failed to seize opportunities because workers weren't aware of their colleagues' expertise. For this reason, we focused on ways managers can improve a network's ability to sense and respond to new opportunities. Rather than map information flow, we set out to assess a latent view of a network's potential to react in the face of new problems or opportunities. By *latent* we mean the people who might be tapped when circumstances change (and not necessarily those who are now being sought for information).

Through interviews with managers and surveys conducted across a series of organizations, we consistently found two aspects of relationships that identify the people whom others seek out when faced with new opportunities or challenges.[1] First, knowing and valuing what another person knows dictates whether and why you will seek out that individual for information or help. Even if all aspects of organizational design support collaboration, people won't connect on new projects if they are unaware of each other's skills and expertise. The second predictor is the seeker's ability to gain timely access to that person. Knowing that someone has relevant expertise does little good if you cannot get access to his or her thinking in a timely fashion.

These two relational dimensions can be mapped to provide a latent view of a network—not the people currently being tapped for information but the people who might be tapped when circumstances change. In this way, managers can discover precise ways to improve a network's ability to leverage members' expertise. For example, if you discover that the problem is lack of awareness, it might make sense to consider a skill-profiling system or new staffing practices—technical and social initiatives designed to help a network know what it knows. If access is a problem, it might make sense to consider peer feedback or technical means of connecting distributed workers, such as video conferencing or instant messaging.

Awareness Networks

Mapping the awareness of "who knows what" in a group gives you insight into the potential for members to tap the expertise of their colleagues. For example, we analyzed a network of scientists in a pharmaceutical company (not the same one described in chapter 2). To deliver a high-quality compound in a timely fashion, this new-product development team needed to integrate highly specialized knowledge about drug development. But members of the group were dispersed across five geographic sites and four hierarchical levels, and they were attempting to bring together very different kinds of expertise.

One telling view of this network emerged when we analyzed who understood and valued whose expertise in the network. We found that what we call the *awareness network* was very sparse compared with others we had seen. This indicated that group members were unfamiliar with their colleagues' abilities and were not exploiting the best expertise that was on the team. Two characteristics of this group explained why. First, the physical separation precluded serendipitous interactions that often reveal people's expertise. Second, the group's specialists struggled to find common ground with colleagues from other specialties. Even when opportunities arose to integrate various kinds of expertise, one group of specialists often did not know enough about what other specialists did to find a way to involve them.

Various initiatives can help increase awareness of who knows what. On a technical front, skill-profiling systems and other collaborative forums can promote this awareness. British Telecom, for example, realized that its global effort to expand product lines and services was hampered because each of its six industry sectors had become a silo. Employees were not aware of the knowledge and expertise of employees in the other sectors. To overcome this lack of awareness and improve cross-sector collaboration, the company introduced virtual communities of practice that were connected through the Knowledge Interchange Network (KIN). This distributed technology helped increase members' awareness of expertise and improved cross-sector collaboration.

Other companies and government organizations have focused more on face-to-face interaction through such forums as *knowledge fairs*, where teams or departments distribute information about what they do. Although the scope of such initiatives is limited, they can help increase awareness of expertise throughout an organization as well as current projects that might be relevant but unknown to others. For example, the World Bank made a strategic decision to reposition itself from a lending organization to a provider of knowledge and services. For its employees to meet the needs of its member organizations, the bank needed to increase awareness of the expertise throughout the organization, and knowledge fairs were a critical part of this process. People from each thematic group set up booths to inform others of their expertise.

Other organizations use staffing or rotation programs as cost-effective ways to create awareness across critical network divides. For example, Aventis, a pharmaceutical company formed by the merger of Rhône-Poulenc and Hoechst, employs the GET (Global Experience Transfer) program to help create awareness of expertise and concerns between their marketing and R&D organizations. Selected employees from the R&D and marketing functions of specific therapeutic units are paired and go through a rotation program in each other's functional unit (with each employee alternating in the mentoring role). This process helps develop a shared context and integrates awareness networks at a critical functional boundary.

Access Networks

When we need help and advice, we often need it right away. Understanding who is accessible to whom (and to what degree) is critical to a network's ability to respond to new opportunities. Typically, access exists along a continuum. At one end of the extreme are people we simply cannot get to, almost always because they are too powerful or too busy. This lack of access can't really be addressed by technology. In the middle of the continuum are people who respond briefly, providing a bare minimum of information or pointers to other sources of information. These interactions can be helpful when we need surface-level information or know a lot about the topic. But when we are wrestling with an issue that is complex or new to us, these people are often not helpful enough for us to use the expertise they share.

At the other end of the continuum are people who engage with us and are truly helpful in more ambiguous information searches. Rather than respond off the cuff, these people help seekers by understanding their requests and responding with actionable insights. This help does not necessarily require much of the expert's time. Rather, engaging in this way is a two-step process in which the person first works to understand the seeker's needs and then shapes what he or she knows to meet those needs. One interviewee put it this way:

> Some people will give you their opinion without trying to either understand what your objectives are or understand where you are coming from, or they will be very closed in their answer to you. But [she] is the sort of person who first makes sure she understands what the issue is. I have been around people who give you a quick spiel because they think they are smart and that by throwing some framework or angle up they can quickly wow you and get out of the hard work of solving a problem. [She], for all her other responsibilities and stature within the firm, is not like that.

As with the awareness network, we have found it helpful to map the *access network* to understand who can reach whom. For example, a network analysis of a group of engineers in a U.S. government agency revealed a well-connected awareness network but a highly fragmented access network. The access network showed considerable grouping by division and was also highly constrained by leaders at the agency's headquarters. As a result, people in this agency were ineffective at leveraging colleagues' expertise because they could not get a response from others in a timely fashion.

To improve the access network—and overall connectivity—the agency managers did two things. First, they conducted a series of group development activities to build social ties across divisions. At quarterly meetings they held fun activities that focused on work topics but also helped build a sense of trust and camaraderie between people who had never worked together. Second, the managers began measuring employees' knowledge sharing in annual performance evaluations. Leaders within the group also encouraged cross-division collaboration and were given leeway to reward this behavior publicly.

If access to the right people can be difficult in the best of times, consider how challenging it can be during a reorganization, when all is in flux. We worked with a mortgage lending organization that was making a transition from a functional to a cross-functional team-based structure to minimize inefficiencies in lending. Before the transition, functional employees were able to tap one another's knowledge rather easily. After the redesign, it became far more difficult for inexperienced people to learn the basics of their functions and for experienced lenders and analysts to solve problems collaboratively.

Network maps showed that four months after the transition to teams, several of the most well-regarded employees were seen as inaccessible by their colleagues. It turned out that these people were being heavily sought out by their past functional colleagues as well as by their new team members, and as a result they were falling behind in their own work. In the functional department, managers had been able to observe such information seeking, but in the team-based environment it was difficult for them to see how instrumental these opinion leaders had become. In fact, a cursory review of individual performance metrics (such as loans serviced or loans booked) revealed that these experts had experienced a significant decline in productivity. Further, the longer hours they were working—in tandem with declining performance metrics, which influenced their bonuses—were undermining their morale.

As people increasingly work from different locations, organizations are struggling with the issue of accessibility. Most have implemented technical solutions, such as e-mail, asynchronous and synchronous collaborative environments, video conferencing, and instant messaging. We find, however, that companies that focus only on technology may be ignoring organizational design considerations and cultural norms, which are more powerful ways to promote accessibility.

Performance management systems that promote individualistic behaviors seem to be one of the primary causes of sparse, disconnected networks. Hierarchy, too, often has a marked impact on who has access to whom. Some organizations have taken steps, such as making knowledge sharing a part of the mission or code of ethics, to promote access across the hierarchy. At Buckman Laboratories, all associates are empowered to speak with any associate at any level, and this is supported by a communication technology that gives each employee access to all others.

Organizations are also considering how the layout of physical space promotes planned as well as serendipitous interactions. For example, Chrysler has gone full circle: from dispersion back to co-location. All the people involved in new car development have been brought into one building so that they can have face-to-face access to one another. Alcoa's new headquarters has open offices, family-style kitchens in the center of each floor, and plenty of open spaces. Before the new design, top executives interacted only with a few people in the elevator and those with whom they had scheduled meetings. Now executives bump into each other more often and are more accessible to all employees for serendipitous conversations. This change in space layout has increased general accessibility and has narrowed the gap between top executives and employees.

Others have built accessibility into work management practices. British Petroleum, for example, recognized that collaborative problem solving is especially crucial during the early stages of a project, when learning from the experience of others can have a disproportionate impact on the project's trajectory and success. As a result, the company instituted a peer review process for drilling initiatives. A project manager is required to invite peers to provide input before major tasks get under way, and the peers, in turn, are required to respond to these requests. Because the focus is on performance, those with the most relevant knowledge and recent experience are tapped to participate. In this way, performance on the task at hand improves and people become more aware of others' abilities.

A Combined Network View

In addition to assessing the knowledge and access networks separately, managers can look at a combination of these networks to improve their understanding of a network's potential to respond to new opportunities. For example, in the same firm as the knowledge-management consultants described at the beginning of this chapter, we conducted a social network analysis of thirty-eight telecommunications consultants. We first assessed employees' awareness to better understand who in this group indicated that they knew and valued others' expertise (see figure 3-2a). The diagram took on new life, however, when we overlaid the access network (figure 3-2b). Ultimately, both knowledge and access must be present for information sharing to be effective. By combining these two networks, we had a view of the potential of a person to obtain information from others when faced with a new problem or opportunity.

Several things were interesting in this combined network. First, we noticed a marked decline in connectivity compared with the awareness network alone. Promoting effective networks requires attention to

FIGURE 3-2a

Awareness Network

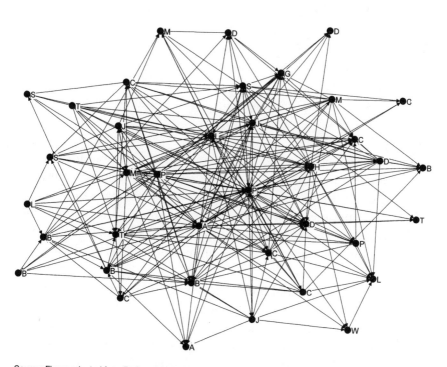

Source: Figure adapted from R. Cross and L. Prusak, "The Political Economy of Knowledge Markets in Organizations," in *Blackwell Handbook of Organizational Learning and Knowledge Management,* eds. M. Lyle and M. Easterby-Smith (Oxford, UK: Blackwell, 2003).

FIGURE 3-2b

Combined Awareness and Access Network

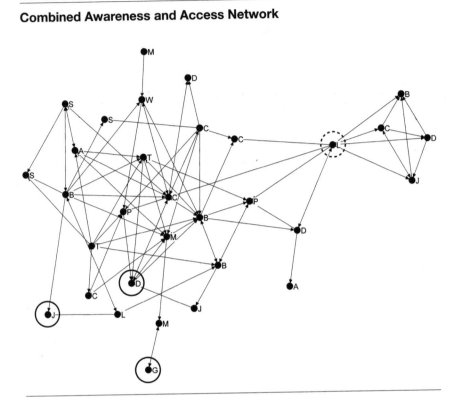

both awareness and access. It is one thing to build an awareness of who knows what in a network. It is another to create a social context in which these relationships are helpful. One reason that skill-profiling systems have not been more successful is that sought-after people often do not respond. If incentives, culture, leadership, or time run counter to one person helping another, no amount of technical infrastructure can solve the problem.

Second, we discovered interesting roles in the combined network. For example, the partners in the group (denoted by solid circles in figure 3-2b) shifted to the periphery. In general, as people move higher in an organization, their work becomes more administrative, and that makes them less accessible and less knowledgeable about the day-to-day work of their subordinates. When we added the access dimension, the people who remained central were all midlevel managers. Although not high in the formal chain of command, these people were extremely important in helping colleagues solve novel problems and drive innovation for the group.

Finally, it is interesting to note the subgroup shown on the right side of the network in figure 3-2b. The mere existence of a subgroup is not necessarily a bad thing. On the one hand, a group that has splintered off from the main network can represent untapped knowledge or, occasionally, political problems that must be addressed. On the other hand, to develop new products or services, management might make room and time for people to innovate on the fringe, as General Motors did with its Saturn division or IBM with development of the PC at Boca Raton.

This was the case with the telecommunications consultants. Roughly one year before our analysis, a midlevel manager (L) had been asked to develop a new service line in a technical network application. He immediately hired several uniquely skilled people and began developing the service offering and sales opportunities. Over time, the smaller group became isolated from the main group. This was not necessarily bad given the group's charter, but it was a problem that this group was linked to the main network through only one person. When this person (L) was lured away by a high-tech start-up, the small group was left in a vulnerable, isolated position. While the consulting practice was able to integrate these people over time, many billable hours were lost in the process.

Taking a combined network view can help an organization understand why people are peripheral and thus find the appropriate solution. You need to take different steps when you're dealing with a person who is peripheral because others do not know about his or her knowledge and skills than when you're dealing with a person who is inaccessible.

Mapping these relationships can also help managers improve the effectiveness of virtual networks. In a study with Steve Borgatti at Boston College, we found that awareness and access statistically mediate the relationship between physical proximity and information seeking.[2] In other words, close physical proximity leads to awareness and access, which in turn leads to information seeking in networks. This suggests that in addition to face-to-face meetings, other initiatives can help virtual workers connect with colleagues. Although virtual workers will still not have the kind of serendipitous information sharing that occurs at the coffee machine, improving awareness and access in networks can lead to greater collaboration.

Types of Information and Problem-Solving Networks

Whom we seek out in a given situation is also a product of what we need. So far we have considered information flow to be one-dimensional. But in reality, various kinds of information often move within a network, and on occasion it can be worthwhile to assess specific kinds of information relevant to a group's success. Far too frequently, managers automatically equate networks with communication. But it is not clear what you are getting if you analyze a communication network using a single question, such as, Whom do you typically communicate with?

Often, the central people in a communication network are secretaries and office managers. To be sure, these people play critical coordinating roles. But less often are they central to strategic aspects of the group's work, such as generating new business, solving complex problems, or devising new products. It is always important to remember that communication networks pick up, to some degree, jokes, gossip, administrative detail, and personal conversations. Of course, we expect more than just information to flow in healthy networks. The point is not to eliminate non–work-related interactions but to be precise in the relationships we map so that we clearly see the means and business benefits of improving collaboration.

When it makes sense, we push companies to define the kinds of information they must share to be successful, and then we analyze each kind of knowledge. For example, in the pharmaceutical example mentioned earlier, we asked employees about various aspects of the compound under development. By asking them to indicate whom they went to for specific types of information about the development, marketing, or promotion of the drug, we pinpointed breakdowns in collaboration between research and sales/marketing on very precise kinds of critical knowledge. This precision also has been very helpful for other organizations, such as hospitals, software development firms, deep-sea drilling, and investment analysts. In each case, the trick is to define what kinds of information need to be shared within the group and then to map each kind as a separate network.

In this vein, managers can use network analysis to assess other important kinds of collaboration. In several cases, we have mapped both an information flow network (whom do you turn to for information to get your work done?) and a problem-solving or brainstorming network (whom do you typically turn to for help in thinking through a new or challenging problem at work?). Problem-solving networks can identify experts and a capacity for innovation in ways that information flow diagrams do not.

For example, problem-solving networks can be crucial in mergers or restructurings, when groups are being brought together to integrate what they know. Consider figure 3-3a. Here we see two sets of research scientists. To integrate world-class expertise, a large company (the square nodes represent scientists from this company) acquired a much smaller company (the circular nodes). Six months after the acquisition, we assessed both information flow and problem-solving networks. The results, as shown in figure 3-3b, were telling. Although information flowed fairly freely in the network, there were much fewer problem-solving interactions, and those that did exist tended to cluster according to the previous boundaries of the two companies.

FIGURE 3-3a

Recently Merged Researchers: Information Network

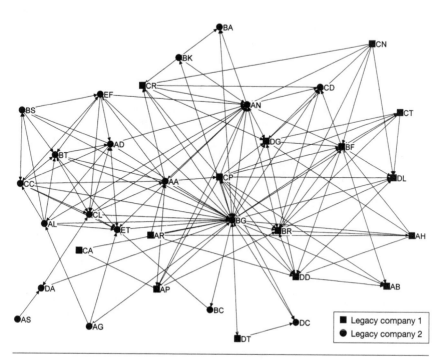

FIGURE 3-3b

Recently Merged Researchers: Problem-Solving Network

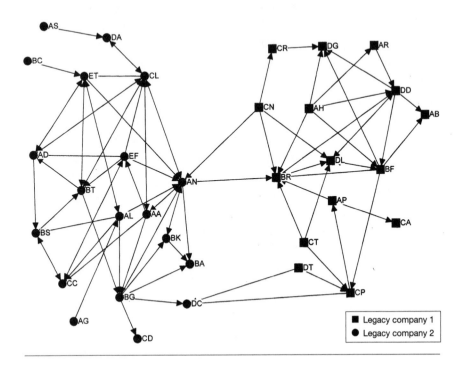

■ Legacy company 1
● Legacy company 2

This is common. If workers know roughly what they need to find out, they are likely to turn to the person they think has relevant information. But in solving novel or unstructured problems, most of us are more selective. We hope that those who shape our thinking really know something about the topic, but this is difficult to ascertain when we ourselves may not know a great deal in novel situations. We also tend to trust these people, because brainstorming often demands that we admit a lack of knowledge and take risks with ideas. Trust often takes time to develop but clearly has substantial implications in knowledge-intensive work.

In our studies, people did not necessarily need to trust experts in order to seek them out for surface information, but they did need to trust them for the exchange to be one where true learning took place. This is particularly true when people are dealing with new projects. In chapter 6 we discuss how to promote trust in relationships. As with networks in general, we don't necessarily suggest that investing in developing more trusting relationships is always a prudent use of time and money. However, when people are dealing with complex problems and novel solutions, establishing trust can have a substantial impact on the quality of collaboration.

Knowing What We Know

Effective networks often entail more than information flow. Groups that need to be highly responsive to customers benefit greatly from improving everyone's awareness of and access to expertise. It's also important for managers to assess the kinds of interactions that occur, from surface information to deep problem solving. A network perspective offers precise information that can guide an executive's efforts to improve the flexibility and effectiveness of employee groups.

But managing information is only part of the battle. We can have a good, or at least good enough, solution but not be able to get others to see and take action on our point of view. Some people are particularly effective at generating energy or enthusiasm for their ideas, an ability that makes them highly influential and productive. We turn next to the idea of energy and explore how it is created and moves in networks.

4

Charged Up

Creating Energy in Organizations

Our high performers are not just people who are smart. We have some of the brightest consultants in the world here. But some are more successful than others, and it has much more to do with what I call buzz than a slight difference in IQ. Our high performers create enthusiasm for things. I mean they are smart and have good ideas, but more than that they are able to get people to buy into and take action on their ideas. They create energy, and even though this is intangible it generates client sales and follow-on work as well as gets other people here engaged in and supportive of what they are doing. I know this might sound like a New Age idea, but what I call buzz or energy has a lot to do with these people's and ultimately the firm's success.

—Managing partner at a strategy consulting firm

THIS PARTNER'S insight came as we were conducting a network analysis at a well-known strategy consulting firm. At the time, we were working with several organizations to define networks of high-performing employees. Our thesis was that better performers would be more effective at getting information to solve problems at work. As a result, we were profiling employees in terms of individual expertise, use of technology, and ability to get information from their networks both within and outside the organization. That is, until this partner's comment pushed us to think a little differently.

His point was that getting information and having a good idea are only a part of what makes many high performers successful. These people have good ideas, but they are also good at convincing customers, team members, and their bosses of the merit of their thinking. Most of us have been in situations where the best idea, maybe our own, did not win out. We might even walk away shaking our heads, wondering why others didn't see the brilliance of our thoughts. People who create energy, this partner was suggesting, may have this experience less than most because they are more effective at getting others enthused about and willing to support their ideas.

After this meeting, we added a question to our survey to see who energized whom in this organization. The network maps from our energy question were compelling. By looking at clustering in the *energy network*, we were quickly able to pick out several projects that were considered highly successful because of the innovative solutions they had generated. The clustering also identified leaders, formal and informal, who were high performers. And we found some people on the periphery of these networks who—no surprise—left the organization before we even had time to analyze and present our results.

By looking at the de-energizing relationships, we also found a dark side to energy. Most of us know people who have an uncanny ability to drain the life out of a group. When possible, we avoid them, often at the expense of not capitalizing on their expertise. When we do have to engage with them, the negative effect usually extends beyond the specific interaction. We are likely to spend time dreading a meeting and mentally rehearsing how we will cope with the de-energizer. The interaction itself is usually unproductive and disheartening. And afterward, we often feel deflated and seek out colleagues with whom we can vent our frustration. Unfortunately, de-energizers not only drain the people they meet but also affect the productivity of people they may not even know.

In the network we analyzed, most of the de-energizing relationships belonged to the group's managers. Sharing this information with the leadership team was, to say the least, delicate. Yet to their credit the leaders immediately asked us to conduct interviews to help them understand how their styles and interactions with others were depleting energy. Identifying specific behaviors would allow them to engage in coaching and development as well as embed these behaviors more deeply into HR practices within the organization (such as hiring and

360-degree feedback). To be sure, the leaders did not expect to be ener-gizing to everyone all the time. Sometimes leadership requires making tough, unpopular decisions. However, they were keenly aware that energy was intricately intertwined with leadership. In the past, and oc-casionally during recessions, authoritarian styles might win the day. But to retain high performers who have many options, these executives needed to consider leadership in terms of managing energy in them-selves and others.

How Energy Affects Performance and Learning

Once we were attuned to the idea of energy, we found it hard to go through a day at any organization without hearing the term used fre-quently. For example, projects are often characterized as having high or low energy, and the high-energy projects are where things are getting done. Alternatively, influential people are often described as being able to create energy and support for initiatives they are involved with. Our experience with the consulting firm made it clear that energy is closely tied to how ideas get put into action. But even though energy is perva-sive in organizations, it is also elusive. We wondered how energy was created and transferred in groups and whether it truly related to orga-nizational performance or learning.

We set out to address these questions by using network analysis. Although energy might be derived from intrinsic motivation or in-spired by job design, we were interested in how it is generated in day-to-day interactions at work. We assessed energy in seven large groups in different organizations by using social network analysis techniques to map relationships in each group. Specifically, we asked this question: "When you interact with this person, how does it typically affect your energy level?" Respondents indicated a value from 1 to 5, where 1 meant strongly de-energizing and 5 indicated strongly energizing.[1]

Assessing energy in networks can be highly illuminating. You can discover, for example, which people are "attractors" in the organization. You can determine which projects generate the most enthusiasm and so have the greatest likelihood of success. You can find out whether reor-ganizations or other large-scale changes are having the desired effect.

For example, in a government agency we assessed, new executives had been brought in to mobilize support for a new set of priorities among a nationally distributed network of executives after the September 11 terrorist attacks. How do you know whether such executive shifts are effective? One way is to assess the engagement of the network as a whole. Energizing relationships in this network, captured in figure 4-1, combined with a series of interviews, clearly revealed that the leaders were effective in engaging others in the agency's new strategic direction.

Managers can also look for energy sappers. A de-energizer may be an individual who can be counseled or coached in various ways, or may be a category of people, such as members of a functional area or a group of leaders. Are critical strategic initiatives capturing employees'

FIGURE 4-1

Energizing Leaders in a Government Agency

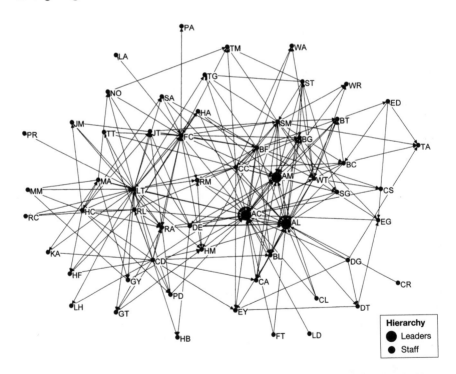

Source: Figure adapted with permission of the publisher. From W. Baker, R. Cross, and M. Wooten, "Positive Organizational Network Analysis and Energizing Relationships," in *Positive Organizational Scholarship,* copyright © 2003 by K. Cameron, J. Dutton, and R. Quinn. Berrett-Koehler Publishers, Inc., San Francisco, CA. All rights reserved. <www.bkconnection.com>.

attention? Are there splits across functional domains of a network because people are enthusiastic about different aspects of their work or are propelled in different directions by performance metrics? Is leadership itself draining the life from a group? A group of engineers within a petrochemical organization we assessed indicated that many of them found their supervisors to be de-energizing (see figure 4-2). In fact, when the supervisors are removed from the network map, the number of de-energizing connections drops by 91 percent. Here, insights revealed by the energy network uncovered unique perspectives on leadership and formed the basis of feedback, coaching, and development processes critical to improving morale.

FIGURE 4-2

De-Energizing Leaders in a Petrochemical Organization

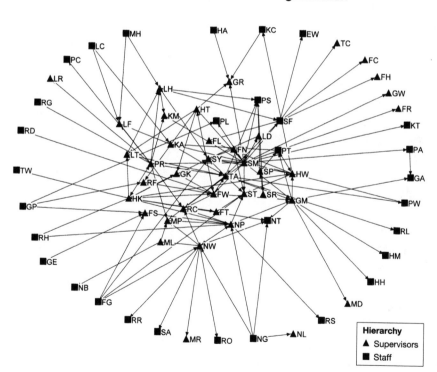

Individual Performance and Learning

But does energy really matter for individual performance or learning? In three of the seven organizations, we obtained reliable performance information on the people in the energy network. We found a critical link between a person's position in the network and his or her performance as measured by annual human resource ratings.[2] In all surveys, we assessed information flow in the entire network as well as each person's use of impersonal sources such as files and databases. We anticipated that those who tapped their informational environment more effectively would be better performers. Intriguingly, we found in all three settings that performance was closely connected to people's positions in the energy network. Even after accounting for the use of various personal and impersonal sources of information, we found that those who energized others were much higher performers.

Social network research suggests that people gain knowledge and power by occupying specific positions in a network. Those who bridge relatively disconnected pockets of a network are promoted earlier and are more mobile in their careers because they hear about opportunities before others do. Our results suggest that those who energize others may be more likely to be heard and to have their ideas put into action. Good or at least feasible ideas are abundant in organizations. Having an epiphany is no big deal unless you can motivate others to believe in it and act on it. Energizers are better at getting others to act on their ideas within organizations, such as garnering support for initiatives, and outside organizations, such as persuading clients to purchase consulting services or software.

Our interviews also suggest that energizers get more from those around them. In the short term, people devote themselves more fully in interactions with an energizer, giving undivided attention in a meeting or problem-solving session. People are also more likely to devote discretionary time to an energizer's concerns. Reflecting on a problem during our commute, sending an extra e-mail or two to find information, or introducing someone to a valued contact are all things we are much more likely to do for an energizer than for a de-energizer.

All things being equal, energizers also win out in the internal labor market by attracting other high performers. Reputation spreads quickly, and in all but the most bureaucratic organizations, people position themselves to work for those who are engaging. Few people would jockey to work for a de-energizer. And this desire to work for or with energizers seems to account for our final finding about energy and performance: Not only were energizers better performers, but people who were closely connected to energizers were also better performers. In other words, energizers raise the overall level of performance around them.

Energizers also have a striking impact on what individuals and groups learn over time. People rely on their networks for information to get their work done. When we have a choice, however, we are much more likely to seek information and learn from energizers than de-energizers.

For example, two network views of a group of government executives are shown in figures 4-3a and 4-3b. Figure 4-3a reflects the information-seeking network in this group. The more interesting view occurs in figure 4-3b, where we see a combination of the de-energizing and information-seeking networks. This diagram shows the extent to

FIGURE 4-3a

The Effect of Energy on Learning: Information-Seeking Network

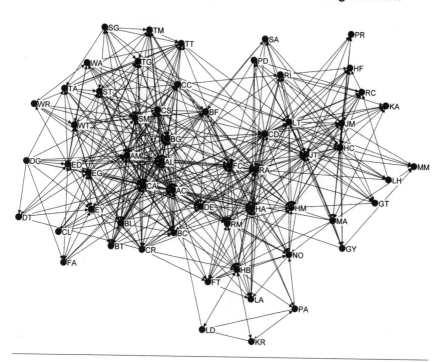

FIGURE 4-3b

The Effect of Energy on Learning: Information-Seeking Relationships with De-Energizers

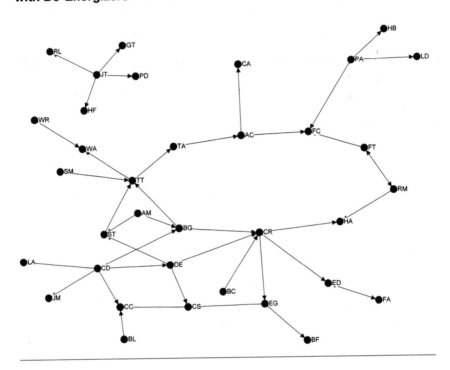

which people seek information from de-energizers. In other words, a line exists only when a member of this group claims to seek information from a de-energizer. The drop-off in connectivity graphically illustrates the extent to which people avoid de-energizers. Moreover, all the links except two were formal reporting relationships that required people to turn to a specific de-energizer for information.

Everyone in our interviews acknowledged this without missing a beat. When we have a choice, which is more often than we might think, we seek out energizers. As a result, these people have a disproportionate effect on what a group learns. On the other end of the scale, the expertise of de-energizers often goes untapped no matter how relevant it might be. And, problematically, instead of finding ways to modify their behavior, de-energizers tend to persist in unconstructive approaches when they are bypassed. In the words of one executive, avoiding de-energizers "just makes them yell louder and cause more problems because they don't feel heard. And it can become a crusade for them. They keep pushing their opinions harder, rather than trying different ways to constructively engage the group, and the whole thing just spirals down from there. No matter how smart they are, they get increasingly counterproductive and are overlooked by the group, which, again, seems to make them push harder in the wrong way."

A Grounded View of Energy in Social Networks

In light of the substantial performance and learning implications of energizing relationships, we engaged in qualitative research to understand how energy is created in interactions with others. Using a case-based approach, we conducted interviews with people from each of the seven social networks we assessed (interviewing three people from each hierarchical level). The interviews were semistructured and required interviewees to discuss interactions and relationships with people they had identified as either energizing or de-energizing. Throughout, we were specifically interested in understanding how energy is created (in interactions with energizers) or destroyed (in interactions with de-energizers).

Two themes emerged. First, energizing interactions are clearly influenced by people's *behavior,* but they are also influenced by certain *characteristics* of the individuals and the relationships between them. For example, two people—one trusted and one not trusted—can exhibit the same behaviors in a conversation but with different results. Similarly, people can be energized by the vision of someone who has integrity and stands for more than his or her own personal gain. Yet the same vision articulated by someone without integrity can be highly de-energizing. Thus, energy is not entirely a product of a set of behaviors in a given interaction but is also affected by people's day-to-day actions.

Second, energy is created in conversations that balance several dimensions of an interaction. Energizing conversations often revolve around a vision or goal, which must be compelling enough to capture people's aspirations but not so grand that it is seen as infeasible or so daunting that it creates stress. And a conversation must be focused enough so that there is a sense of progress but not so much that people feel constrained or irrelevant. In short, energy lives in a sweet spot in five dimensions of conversations or group problem-solving sessions: a compelling goal, the possibility of contributing, a strong sense of engagement, the perception of progress, and the belief that the idea can succeed. Hitting the midpoint of these dimensions, not the extremes, is the challenge for those who want to inspire energy.

These prescriptions might appear obvious, but in practice they often fall by the wayside for leaders caught up in demanding work environments. In fact, we heard many stories of well-intentioned people who were destroying their careers as leaders by not attending to some of these seemingly simple behaviors. In settings where your ability to engage others is critical and authoritarian approaches are ineffective, these behaviors have a lot to do with whether work gets done as you might hope when you are not present. Several organizations we work with have incorporated these behaviors into human resource practices such as hiring, employee development, and performance evaluation. Such efforts help build energizing environments beyond the results of a given interaction or leader.

Now let's look at these five dimensions in detail.

A Compelling Vision

Energy usually is not generated in conversations about current or past problems. Such discussions may provide a foundation for a compelling vision and may alleviate tension created by uncertainty, but in the absence of a compelling vision, they do not create energy. Whether in the pursuit of personal or business objectives, energy is produced from a focus on possibilities or, in the words of one interviewee, "what *could be* rather than what is or what has been." Possibilities, or visions, must be worthy of people's time and effort, but they cannot be overwhelming. Interviewees consistently indicated that conversations about infeasible projects were highly de-energizing. They often left such interactions annoyed that they had wasted time or distressed by the amount of work they had inherited.

The ability to create a compelling vision, either by articulating it well or building it through conversations, was a consistent point of difference between energizers and de-energizers. Energizers see realistic possibilities; de-energizers see roadblocks at every turn. This is not to say that disagreement or constructive conflict is inherently de-energizing. Almost all interviewees indicated that energizing people were quick to point out potential problems in their effort to advance an idea. But de-energizers disagree or see the negative in a situation as a matter of personality. They exclusively see the things that can go wrong or the reasons that a plan will not work. By frequently airing these opinions, they can have a deadly effect on the ability of a group to create a compelling but realistic future. As a manager said about one of his team members, "He always sees only problems or reasons that we can't do things a certain way. That gets old over time. It's not a single disagreement that kills you; it's the personality behind it—one that is constantly overly critical and nongenerative. But [an energizer] is not like that. He has more of a tendency to see opportunities in situations and really act like they are opportunities. And that's energizing all around. In general, people want to be part of building something."

A Meaningful Contribution

The second feature of energizing interactions is feeling that you have contributed to the creation of a compelling vision or that you have the ability and will contribute to its attainment. Energy is closely intertwined with the belief that your efforts make a difference. Very often you get this sense from others acknowledging or building on your ideas.

For example, one consultant described an energizing manager, "She came into the meeting, and I know she had a thousand other things going on, but she was immediately there and with us. She was listening to what we had done and why, and throughout the interaction was asking good questions. And this is typical of dealing with her on projects. Where others at that level might come in with preconceived plans and totally ignore your work, she always comes in open and willing to listen to what you have done. She shows a value for your effort and ideas that makes you want to do your best there and later."

Energizers create opportunities for people to enter conversations or problem-solving sessions in ways that make them feel heard. They are not blinded by their own thoughts, perspectives, or points of view. In contrast, de-energizers often either do not create the space in a conversation for others to engage or do not find ways to value others' perspectives. This can be a particular problem for people who have a great deal of expertise. Experts, even when offering sound solutions, can bulldoze people, keeping them from contributing at that time and decreasing the likelihood that they will try again in the future.

This is not to say that all contributions made in a conversation or group problem-solving session should be celebrated—only that effective contributions need to be acknowledged and ineffective ones handled in a way that does not marginalize the contributor. Energizers do two things that keep a disagreement from being de-energizing. First, they disclose their own logic for disagreeing and thus allow others to probe and critique their perspectives. This stands in contrast to de-energizers, who often criticize without offering alternatives or exposing their own thinking.

Second, energizers separate the idea they disagree with from the person contributing it. Particularly for those in positions of authority, a critical challenge lies in allowing others to maintain confidence in their thinking and ability to contribute while generating and following up only on the group's best ideas. In their choice of language, de-energizers tend to tie people's contributions tightly to them and, unfortunately, dwell on ideas with which they disagree instead of acknowledging those that are insightful. A de-energizer might approach a disagreement with the following: "You said this, which does not seem like a very good solution. I think . . ." In contrast, an energizer might begin with a more neutral approach: "Given what we are trying to accomplish, here is one other route we might consider." The first approach knowingly or un-knowingly makes a value statement tightly linked with the contributor. It also creates a situation in which participants must choose between proposals rather than seek out integrative solutions. In contrast, the energizer focuses on the ideas, opens a set of new possibilities, and does not marginalize a group member in the process.

Full Engagement

A third hallmark of energizing interactions, in either two-party conver-sations or group problem-solving sessions, is that participants are fully present in the conversation. This means first understanding what oth-ers are saying and then appropriately bringing knowledge and expertise to the discussion. Energy seems to accrue as people simultaneously contribute and hear the insights of others similarly engaged. Having to reach out to nonparticipants can be de-energizing as well as distracting. And having to respond to comments that reveal a person's inattention has a similar impact.

People can be drained by interactions demanding such mental in-tensity. Humor, in the form of funny stories or quips, often helps peo-ple refresh themselves and refocus. It also allows people to engage with others apart from their roles and thus reestablish a genuine sense of connection. But excessive humor takes people off track. And, of course, humor that others don't appreciate often encourages them to withdraw from a group or conversation.

A key characteristic of engagement also involves your physical actions. Body language can signal and inspire energy through subtle but important cues, such as eye contact, leaning into a conversation, speaking in an animated way, hand gestures, or writing on a white board. And consider the signals that are sent by someone who does not make eye contact, continually checks the time, speaks in a monotone or sounds exasperated, peers out the window, or repeatedly answers their cell phone. One executive described someone who knew how to engage others: "He is unbelievable. It is hard to describe, but it is just a sheer force he seems to exert that you feed off of. In terms of body language he is animated and engaged with you. He is also listening and reacting to what you are saying in a rich way. Not many people do that. They kind of listen but with an eye to how they can advance their own points, or maybe they go through the motions of listening but you know they are thinking about something else."

Note that energizers are not entertainers, or even necessarily very charismatic or intense. Rather, they bring themselves fully into a given interaction. If the phone rings, they choose not to answer it. They don't let their minds wander to topics that are more interesting to them and so signal lack of interest by comments or questions that show they have not been attentive. Although it is easy to believe we can do many tasks at once, in reality most of us give off all sorts of indicators when we are not paying attention even if we are only rarely confronted about this.

A Sense of Progress

Energizing interactions feel as if they are leading somewhere. As a result, the way a conversation evolves is critical to generating a sense of energy. On the one hand, unfocused problem solving or a great many unresolvable problems can drain energy from an interaction. People do not have to leave every interaction with a solution, but they must leave at least knowing which steps to take. On the other hand, problem-solving sessions that are too focused or too driven toward one person's (often the leader's) solution are also de-energizing. People need to believe that their thoughts matter. If people feel that the answer is predetermined or that only some people's voices are heard (perhaps those at a certain hierarchical level or those whom the leader likes), they will quickly disengage.

Energizers are driven to a goal but are open and flexible regarding the process. De-energizers often don't provide sufficient structure (or resist what others are trying to establish) and so create contexts where no sense of progress can be enjoyed. Or they might enforce excessive structure or preconceptions of the right course of action and in doing so marginalize the work and thoughts of others. For example, a software developer told this story: "We had been working like crazy on this project when he swooped in and just started telling us what we should do. He didn't take the time to try to understand what we were telling him or even care about the work we had done. That not only crushed the ideas that could have been developed in that session but also kept people from caring and putting in any more effort than they had to going forward."

Belief in the Goal

Finally, there is an emotional aspect to energy, but perhaps not in the way you might immediately think. Our interviews made it clear that most of us can be energized by people we do not like or by tasks we may not initially find engaging. In such situations, emotion seems to enter the fray by way of hope. In a very real sense, people allow themselves to be energized when they begin to believe that the objective being established in a conversation is worthy and can be attained. Rather than observing an interaction—remaining removed, distant, or judgmental—people become energized when they let themselves get excited about the possibilities and stop looking for all the things that can go wrong.

This decision to let go of reservations—to hope—is influenced by the energizer. In particular, an energizer's integrity has an impact on energy creation (or depletion) in two important ways. First, energizers speak their minds rather than harbor hidden agendas or act the way they should based on their role in the organization. People feel that they get the truth from energizers even when it is not necessarily pleasant. In contrast, political behaviors are a sure way to destroy energy. Such behaviors might include posturing, agreeing excessively with a person in a higher position, or collaborating with others in a political fashion, thus creating alliances or cliques. In any case, energy is depleted when ideas begin to be indexed not by their merit but by whom one is agreeing or disagreeing with.

A manager in the strategy consulting firm indicated this: "She just does the right thing. She does things that are about more than just the easy way or the things that would benefit her the most. In one critical meeting, even when we could have gotten out of the client meeting and satisfied them by backing off of some of our points, she didn't. It was the fact that she both stuck by what we had done and also did not compromise on what she thought was right that was so important."

Second, integrity between words and action is critical. The extent to which energy is created or depleted in an interaction hinges on people's belief that they can rely on others to do what they say they are going to do. In our interviews, we repeatedly heard about situations in which people's hopes were dashed because another person did not come through on his or her commitments. Of course, future interactions with such people are often highly de-energizing. A software developer reflected this: "The first time we got into one of these interactions about a project, I went home ecstatic. I gushed on about the ideas to my husband and literally spent the weekend framing the project. But he never came back to me with anything he said he would, and of course I ended up with all the work. The second time I fell for it again. But now I know better, and these interactions I almost run from even though on the surface, most people, not knowing the history, would be pretty excited about the possibilities."

Eight Decisions That Affect Others' Energy

Are you an energizer or a de-energizer? We often focus on how others affect us, but a powerful shift in perspective lies in considering how our actions affect others. Almost universally, our interviewees indicated that the network analysis and interviews were the first times they had thought systematically about their effect on others. Based on our research, we offer eight questions that will help you understand how your behavior affects the energy of others. We refer to these as decisions that we make many times on most days. Thinking in terms of decisions emphasizes that we can choose, in our interactions with colleagues, to act in ways that promote energy.

The first three decisions establish a relational foundation upon which energy can be created. Whereas a common attribute of de-energizers is a single-minded focus on accomplishing tasks, energizers often accomplish as much or more but do so with attentiveness to the people around them. Energizers think of their work as a balance of tasks and relationships, and this manifests itself daily in myriad decisions and behaviors expressing a genuine concern for others. Stopping to ask someone how he or she is doing (and being truly interested), recalling something important in that person's personal life, or shuffling tasks to accommodate someone are only a few of the small behaviors that seem to come easily for energizers. Of course, these interactions cannot be scripted; they must be genuine. But they do not have to be lengthy—people often described to us five-minute hallway interactions that had a significant impact.

The following are three questions to consider about behaviors that create a foundation for creating energy in your relationships:

- Do you make an effort to weave relationship development into work and day-to-day actions? Even when you feel swamped, do you make time to engage with others as people and not as means to an end? If you have concern for others and make connections outside work-based roles, you promote trust and a belief in your integrity.

- Do you do what you say you are going to do? People are energized by a specific task or goal only if they can believe in the integrity of the other person (or people) involved. When energy is created, people let go of their reservations and allow themselves to become enthusiastic. These reservations fall away only if people can trust that others will follow through on their commitments.

- Do you address tough issues with integrity and sincerity? Do you allow political behavior to creep into decisions or interactions with others? People are energized in the presence of others who stand for something larger than themselves. The energizer often benefits from their pursuit, but the pursuit is focused on doing the right thing and not exclusively on personal gain.

Consistency in behavior builds trust in a relationship and thus a context in which energy can be created. Several simple behaviors expressed in conversations or group settings also distinguish energizers from de-energizers. Although these behaviors seem simple, our interviews revealed that they are not widely followed in organizations. We have been impressed with the way that mapping energy and talking about these ideas in a group creates a language that allows people to discuss de-energizing interactions. All the people we worked with suggested that the ability to make a joke out of being de-energized and then articulating how someone was de-energizing helped people change these behaviors. Some questions to consider include the following:

- Do you look for possibilities or identify only constraints? Do you critique ideas without venturing alternatives or revealing your own thinking? In the extreme, de-energizers see nothing but problems and roadblocks. In a less extreme version, which is particularly prevalent among leaders who are troubleshooting, de-energizers do not acknowledge positive aspects of a situation but choose instead to focus on problems. Either approach overlooks people's contributions and robs them of a belief that their contributions matter.

- When you disagree with someone, do you focus attention on the issue and not on the value of that person's contributions? Excessive, insincere agreement destroys energy, and so can disagreement. Energizers are able to disagree with an idea while not marginalizing the person who presented it.

- Are you mentally and physically engaged in meetings and conversations? Full engagement in a conversation or group problem-solving session is central to energy creation. Rather than go through the motions of being engaged—something that is much more transparent than many de-energizers think— energizers physically and mentally show their interest in the person and the topic of the conversation.

- Are you flexible, or do you force others to come to your way of thinking? Energizers draw people into conversations and projects by finding opportunities for them to contribute. In contrast, de-energizers may seem highly energizing but may be so wrapped up in their own thinking that they do not leave space for others to contribute.

- Do you use your own expertise appropriately? Expertise, if used too aggressively, shuts down innovative thinking and strips others of the opportunity to contribute. Often, experts or leaders destroy energy in their haste to find a solution or in a desire to demonstrate their expertise.

We have found that these eight questions form a powerful diagnostic for addressing points in a network where energy is flagging or nonexistent. At a minimum, the questions can be used as a self-test that we all might consider, either individually or by seeking feedback from colleagues, in relation to our interactions with others. When combined with a social network analysis, this diagnostic can provide a powerful device for two parties (or two categories of people, such as leaders and followers) to use in locating problems in their interactions. The network analysis can pinpoint problem areas, and the eight questions can help de-energizers change their behavior.

In addition, several of the organizations we worked with changed their human resource practices in an effort to inspire energizing behaviors more broadly. Simple changes in hiring criteria or performance evaluation processes can have a systematic impact within an organization beyond what might be found in a specific network.

Building Vibrant Networks

Energy is part of everyday talk and experience in organizational life. It is associated with people's motivation and willingness to exert effort. It also is tightly linked to progress; initiatives described as having energy are usually the ones that are moving forward. Analyzing the energy in social networks can allow managers to identify broad patterns. Once these patterns are revealed, network participants can take actions to create, or at least not to destroy, energy and enthusiasm.

To this point in the book, we have shown that using social network analysis to assess specific kinds of relationships can change how people communicate and how they perform their jobs. To correct unproductive network patterns, managers must make a concerted effort. In part two of this book, we describe strategies you can adopt to improve networks at the individual, relational, and organizational levels.

How Managers
Manage Social
Networks

5

Pinpointing the Problem

Understanding How Individuals Affect a Network

We knew we needed to do a better job of working together, but before the network analysis the tools we had to throw at the problem were largely technical and only increased information flow and connectivity. Just a glance at our network diagram shows that more information or relationships is not universally right for everybody. We had people like myself who were way overloaded and couldn't handle more communication. And we had others out on the periphery who were not able to get to people they needed to, and this was totally an issue of becoming known and trusted in the network—not really a technical solution. The magic of the network analysis was being able to find and then address connectivity issues as appropriate for different people, not just ratchet up expectations for everyone.

> —*Senior executive of a global*
> *manufacturing organization*

THIS SENIOR EXECUTIVE was in charge of more than two hundred technicians who often needed to collaborate to solve electrical and mechanical problems with high-end manufacturing equipment. The problem was that the group was distributed around the globe, making it impossible for the executive to meet everyone or even find a single time when most employees could participate in conference calls.

He relied heavily on e-mail and instant messaging and racked up vast numbers of airline miles, but he was still overloaded and spent a lot of time fighting fires. Although he was trying to create a nonhierarchical organization, he knew he had become a bottleneck. But he had no time, space, or idea how to solve the problem.

A network assessment revealed the extent to which communication overload was consuming him and his direct reports. For example, our analysis revealed that each of the top five managers had more than forty-five people coming to them regularly for information. In fact, when we removed these managers from the network, overall connectivity dropped by almost 20 percent. It quickly became obvious why this small group of leaders was working so hard and yet still felt they were falling further behind. Once these overloaded people were identified, steps were taken to shift parts of their jobs to others in the network. This action reduced the extent to which they were bottlenecks and drew peripheral people into the network.

The network analysis also helped us identify many highly peripheral people who were underutilized and frustrated. These people found it difficult to get help from others in a timely fashion. Also, they were often not heard: Despite participating in conference calls and listing their credentials in an online resume, they were seldom sought out or listened to, and that left them wondering how they would ever advance their careers in that division. A key in this situation was to educate central people on the expertise of the peripheral people so that they knew when to draw them into projects. Additional steps—such as a rotation program, mentoring relationships, new orientation practices, and communication forums—also helped peripheral people integrate more smoothly.

These and other changes balanced out connectivity and improved collaboration, largely because the changes targeted needs of specific people in the network. Before we conducted the network analysis, employees were well aware that the group members were not as responsive or collaborative as they needed to be. Yet they characterized the problem as technical—one that better and more instantaneous connectivity could solve. However, the network analysis showed that the last thing that would work was more connectivity and communication. Rather, by focusing on specific issues in relation to people's positions within the network, the network corrections had a much greater and enduring effect.

Identifying Types of Individuals in the Network

We have found that assessing peoples' positions in a network allows managers to target actions to four kinds of people. First, we often focus on *central connectors*, who have a disproportionate number of direct relations in the network and might be either unrecognized resources or bottlenecks. A second type are *boundary spanners*, who connect a department with other departments in the organization or with similar networks in other organizations. *Information brokers* communicate across subgroups of an informal network so that the group as a whole won't splinter into smaller, less-effective segments. Finally, we focus on *peripheral people*, who might either need help getting better connected or need space to operate on the fringes.

Central Connectors

When people look at a social network diagram, their eyes are naturally drawn to those with the most arrows pointing to them. In figure 5-1, Frank (left), Ian (center), and Steve (bottom right) have the most connections in this network. Elaine (top left) is the head of the department, but, as the lines show, most information seemingly flows through Frank, Ian, and Steve.

The immediate assumption most people make is that being highly central is always good and that central people are extremely valuable to the group. Sometimes this is true, but not always. To develop a more nuanced view of why someone is central and how that person affects the network as a whole, we conduct interviews or facilitate sessions. We generally find two categories of overly central people: the unsung hero and the bottleneck.

The Unsung Hero

Almost universally, certain people end up surprising managers by turning out to be much more central than anyone would have guessed. These people tend to engage selflessly in various aspects of their work and support the group in ways that often go unrecognized. Responding directly to requests for information, engaging in problem solving, providing personal support, and putting people in contact with others are some of the ways that this kind of central person goes above and beyond the requirements of the job to help others. This sort of "invisible

FIGURE 5-1

Uncovering Central Connectors, Boundary Spanners, Information Brokers, and Peripheral Specialists

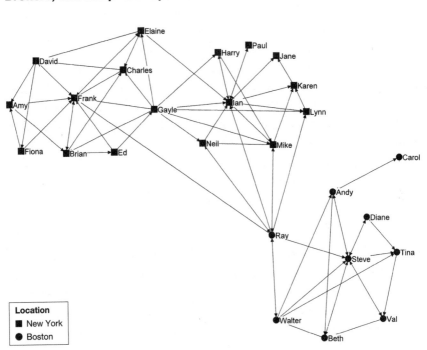

Location
■ New York
● Boston

work" is critical to the network and can consume many hours each day, but it can go completely unrecognized by senior management. As a result, these people are often thrilled to be identified by network analysis because it is usually one of the first times that others see and appreciate their efforts.

The first thing managers can do with these kinds of central connectors is to recognize, encourage, and perhaps reward their contributions to the network. Most organizations are set up to acknowledge and reward individual accomplishments. Thus, people engaging in good citizenship tend to do so of their own volition and often get worn down over time. Publicly acknowledging their contribution motivates them and encourages collaborative behavior among others. It can also be a first step to creating a norm of active cooperation.

Some organizations also offer spot rewards. For example, there were few central connectors at a large engineering company we worked with, so senior executives instituted "above and beyond" rewards: Each time someone went out of his or her way to introduce a colleague in trouble to those who could help, that person was nominated for a small cash reward. The reward was paid out quickly, and the good deed was publicly acknowledged, an incentive that rapidly helped create many more central connectors in the company.

Other organizations have changed aspects of their performance-management systems to regularly reward central connectors. For example, we worked with one investment bank that changed the criteria for annual bonuses. At the end of the review period, each manager's ability to link people in the bank was evaluated by all the people with whom the manager worked. By delineating the collaborative behaviors that central people engage in and then incorporating them into human resource practices, managers can encourage more-collaborative environments and better-connected networks.

The Bottleneck

Some people become so central to a network that they end up holding the group back. Such people tend to take one of two forms. First are those, such as Alam in chapter 3, who play central roles to maintain an informational or power advantage. Social network diagrams can reveal this activity and help facilitate a constructive conversation with the person about changing the behavior. Alternatively, some organizations tackle this problem by changing staffing practices. Using information from a network analysis, executives can staff new teams from subgroups in the network. This approach allows members of different groups to work closely together and lowers the barriers between them. In this way, a manager can break the central connector's stranglehold while still allowing the person to play a key role in the informal network.

The second kind of a bottleneck are people whose jobs have grown too big. They usually work at a frenetic pace to keep up and don't realize that they are slowing others down by not responding quickly enough. In such cases, executives might intervene by reallocating responsibilities. For example, certain people might be central to an informal network because of the depth of their knowledge in consulting or banking or software development. It may be a good idea to reassign some of their other work so that they can focus on their areas of expertise. If people are central only because they monitor information that many people need, it may be possible to make this information more widely available in other ways—for example, using e-mail or a corporate intranet.

Executives often find themselves in this role. One executive we worked with had fifty-three employees who came to her frequently for critical information to get their work done, and another forty-two claiming they would be more effective if they were able to communicate more with her. She was working to her limit but still had become a serious bottleneck for the group. We conducted a two-hour interview with her to get a sense of what was driving her into this position. In the interview, we jointly reviewed, at a high level, meetings stored in her Palm Pilot and recent e-mail correspondence. This helped us quickly define specific kinds of information that she held that could be made available in different formats. We also found decisions that she could let go of, moving some to employees and embedding others (such as approving small expenditures) in policies and procedures.

Although this is an extreme example, we have seen this pattern with leaders in a wide range of networks. An effective way for senior managers to correct the problem is by reallocating information domains (that is, who's responsible for what information) and changing decision rights (allowing others to make decisions).

Boundary Spanners

Boundary spanners provide critical links between two groups of people that are defined by functional affiliation, physical location, or hierarchical level. In figure 5-1, you can see that Ray, one of the members of the informal network on the right, plays a crucial role. Because of his links with Ian (center) and Frank (left), who are central connectors in the New York office of the organization, Ray serves as the main conduit of information between that location and his own. Because Ray is the one who links his group with the outside world, he functions as a boundary spanner. In some settings, a single point of contact between groups is an efficient and effective solution to network integration—better than promoting excessive connectivity.

Boundary spanners play an important role when people need to share different kinds of expertise—for example, in establishing strategic alliances between companies or developing new products. However, boundary spanners are rare because most managers don't have the breadth of expertise, the wealth of social contacts, and the personality traits necessary to be accepted by vastly different groups of people. For example, few marketing managers are welcomed into the heart of an R&D network, largely because the two groups value different aspects of their work. And the organization may not welcome the work of the boundary spanner, who takes up projects and tasks that cut across formal boundaries in the company and thus spends less time in his or her immediate network.

Senior executives can use network maps to check whether boundary spanners are needed or are making the right connections, particularly with central connectors in other groups. In our investment bank example, if Ray were connected only to a peripheral specialist in the New York office (who, by definition, works apart from most colleagues) instead of the two central connectors, the average degree of separation would increase in the network, and some people might be as many as eight removes from others.

It is hard for senior managers to legislate whom the boundary spanner should build relationships with, but they can shape the spanner's networks in subtle ways. At a commercial bank, midlevel managers were asked to set goals for new-product development in conjunction with senior executives in other units. The resulting planning meetings and projects prompted the formation of close relationships among people who served in different functions at different levels of the bank.

A company can reap substantial benefits by recognizing its boundary spanners. Take the case of a consumer goods practice of a global consulting firm we worked with. This group was distributed among offices in North America, Europe, and Australia. Few of the consultants knew their counterparts in other countries, so coordination across the offices was poor. The firm saw a dramatic improvement, however, when it identified the few people who were informally in touch with colleagues in other offices and increasingly assigned them to projects that required travel to offices on all three continents. As a result, the spanners developed larger and more reliable personal networks all over the world. Because the firm was making additional demands on these boundary spanners, the senior partners awarded them salary increases and promoted them quickly. A network analysis conducted a year later showed that many of the groups in the firm were, indeed, much more integrated. New projects were won and old contracts were extended, in part because people could more easily obtain the knowledge and expertise they needed from far-flung colleagues.

Boundary spanners can also play critical roles in large-scale change efforts. For example, we conducted a network analysis of a group of

FIGURE 5-2a

Information Network *with* Five Key Boundary Spanners

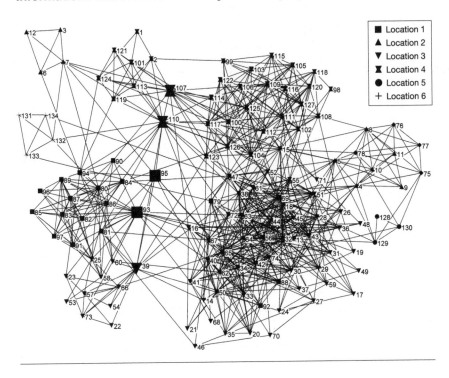

information scientists in a pharmaceutical company. This group had recently been formed through the integration of two separate divisions, each of which had various sites in Europe and the United States. Figure 5-2a, which is coded by location, shows that there is some fragmentation by location within the network but that a few key people link the various sites. When we remove these five critical boundary spanners (figure 5-2b), the split between the groups, and even within some locations, becomes much more substantial. Although spanners may be hidden in large groups, this view shows the extent to which well-placed boundary spanners can promote connectivity within an important network.

Information Brokers

In talking about people's positions in a network, so far we have focused on their direct connections with others. But connections can also be indirect. For example, in figure 5-1, Ian and Frank have no direct

FIGURE 5-2b

Information Network *Without* Five Key Boundary Spanners

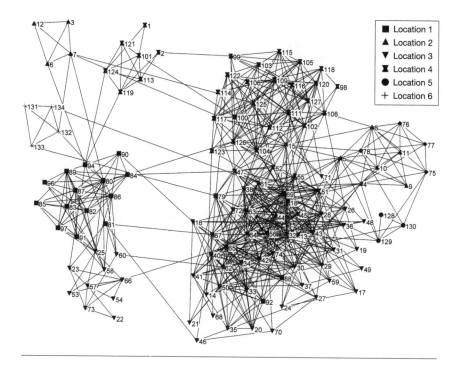

connection, but each has a relationship with Gayle, so they are connected through her. People such as Gayle play a brokering role that can hold together entire groups. By assessing the extent to which a person is close to all others in a network (even people they are not directly connected to) or is sitting on the shortest path between many other people, we can find employees who disproportionately affect information flow.

You can see the importance of information brokers in figures 5-3a and 5-3b. Figure 5-3a shows part of an information network of investment analysts within an oil and gas exploration company, coded by location. We identified the four most prominent brokers in the group; in the diagram these people are identified with larger shapes. Figure 5-3b is the same network with those four people removed. As you can see, with their removal the network becomes much more sparse and fragments into several subgroups.

Targeting information brokers can help an organization disseminate certain kinds of information and promote connectivity throughout

FIGURE 5-3a

Information Network *with* Four Key Brokers

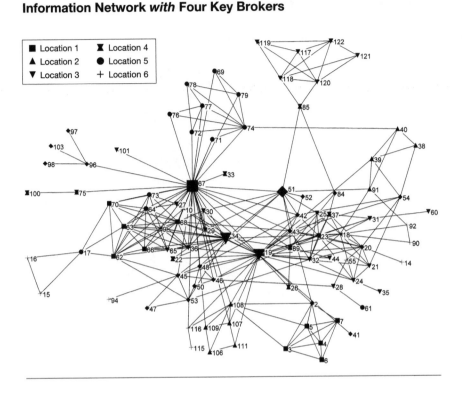

a network. In the above investment analyst community of practice, senior managers set out to develop a more connected network centered on the information brokers. They first identified the top brokers and their expertise, and then they made this expertise explicit to the entire group, indicating whom members should turn to in various situations. They also created bimonthly virtual forums and provided a collaborative technology that helped integrate the brokers and keep them current on who knew (or was doing) what in the network.

These minimal efforts had striking results. The initial social network analysis showed that members of this global community were, on average, four links away from everyone else. After management intervened, members were generally no more than two links away (and never more than three). This is an important level of connectivity to ensure that a group is leveraging its expertise. People are likely to call a friend and maybe even a friend of a friend, but after this the likelihood of continuing a search (or getting a good response) trails off substan-

FIGURE 5-3b

Information Network *Without* Four Key Brokers

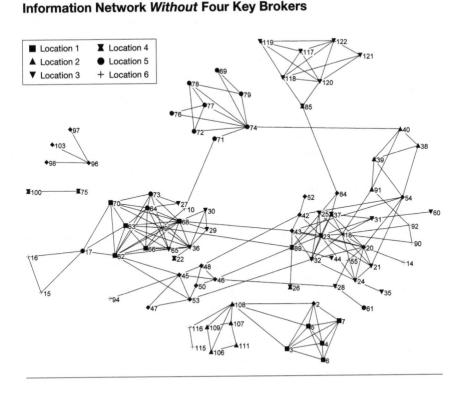

tially. Here the organization increased the likelihood that network members would be able to leverage the expertise of other members with a minimal investment of time or energy.

Peripheral People

Large or small, every informal network has its outsiders, and identifying them is just as important as identifying central or prominent people. Figure 5-1 shows that Paul (center) and Carol (right) operate on the perimeter of this informal network. They have only one connection each and are not linked to each other. The skills, expertise, and unique perspectives of network outliers often are not leveraged effectively, so these people may represent underutilized resources.

Recognizing that a person is isolated from a group is an important first step. As with central people, though, the critical question is this: How is the person affecting the group? People often assume that only those who are worth little to a network end up on the periphery. This may be true if a person's personality or skills just don't fit a group. In such cases, training or a move to another group may be the best solution. We have found, however, that even though people may be on the periphery because of inapplicable skills, quite often they are there because they are either stuck or choose to be peripheral.

Stuck on the Periphery

Some people, particularly those who are new to an organization, may end up on the periphery of a network and have no idea how to work their way inside. Working with such people can yield quick results as they are usually motivated to get more connected and need only a little help.

One way you can help them develop connections is by putting them on internal or external projects with more networked or experienced colleagues. Another approach is to create mentoring relationships or to introduce them to others, whether through formal rotation programs or meetings, to help create awareness of their interests and expertise. And orientation practices that connect new people (rather than just introducing them to their computers and a policy manual) can also be productive, as can simply moving people physically closer to colleagues.

Intentionally Peripheral

There are also people who are on the periphery by choice. For example, experts often fall into this category. Trying to integrate such peripheral yet vital specialists may make it harder for them to stay ahead in their fields; they can't nurture their own expertise if they are forced to sit on committees or meet often with clients.

In one high-tech company we worked with, several of the leading researchers were threatening to resign. Senior management was blindsided by this news because the team had been extremely successful at developing new technologies and introducing them to the rest of the company, and their work had been handsomely rewarded and recognized. But a social network analysis showed that the organization was destroying the group because it did not recognize that most of the scientists were peripheral specialists. As the researchers came up with winning applications, senior managers started asking them to attend more internal meetings and to present their findings to large customers.

Because of their successes, the demands on the researchers' time increased so much that they felt unable to stay at the cutting edge of their expertise, let alone advance it. Management did not recognize that these researchers needed to maintain their peripheral position for their own satisfaction and career success.

People may also operate on the fringes of a network for personal reasons. They might, for example, be their families' primary caregivers. If the company subtly forces them into more activities—such as early-morning conference calls, evening meetings, and increased travel—they will resent having to participate and may eventually quit. Executives who value the expertise of people in these situations need to create room for them to play only peripheral roles in the informal network.

Individual Connectivity in Networks

To this point, we have presented social network analysis as a tool for viewing groups of people. But an equally powerful way to promote connectivity in an organization is to work through each employee's personal network. This benefits the organization as well as the individual. Research has shown that people with more diverse, entrepreneurial networks tend to be more successful. Relationships bridging into subgroups help people find jobs and obtain resources.[1] These relationships are also associated with early promotion, career mobility, and managerial effectiveness.[2] However, many people do not take the time to consider their own networks, or they simply believe that being a good networker is a matter of personality. If you're extroverted and even a bit aggressive, the stereotype goes, you'll end up well connected, almost by definition. If you're more the shy and retiring type, you'll be on the periphery.

Research to date suggests, however, that the link between one's position in a network and personality characteristics is tenuous. In combining many of our social network analyses with personality scales (such as extroversion, Myers-Briggs, FIRO-B, and learning styles), we have found limited and inconsistent relationships between personality traits and network position. Though other scholarly studies have shown some correlation between personality traits and network position,[3] it seems that even the most introverted among us can, and often do, have robust personal networks.

Instead of being a function of personality traits, network centrality seems to reflect how workers think about and engage in work. Our interviews with people in central and peripheral network positions revealed two important characteristics of those who become central more quickly than others. First, central people often seem to structure their work differently. Rather than focus on executing tasks on their own, they seek ways to integrate other people into their work. Second, they systematically take the time to build their own networks. These people always seem to have lists of those they are trying to meet or work with and those to whom they owe calls. To them, building relationships is not a political act but a critical part of professional development, and they continually take specific steps to enrich their networks.

If we shift our perspective and see network patterns not as a product of entrenched personality characteristics but as a result of intentional behaviors, we can discover many opportunities for improving connectivity. In contrast to personality traits, behaviors can be more readily taught or encouraged by an organization's practices. For example, if managers want to get new people up to speed quickly and leverage the expertise of peripheral network members, they can encourage a grassroots approach to network development. Training can help people assess, develop, and support their own networks. Executives can also implement network development in the organization's routines by making it an important component of orientation, professional development, reflective learning activities, and staffing.

Providing employees with a means of planning their personal network development is an effective way to promote connectivity. Such feedback can help employees identify biases in their networks and understand why they might want to invest more in some relationships and less in others. For example, are your subordinates (or you) getting information only from a certain hierarchical level and thus potentially not learning from those lower in the hierarchy (a frequent occurrence)? Alternatively, are they leveraging only those colleagues who are physically close or in the same functional unit, or are they actively reaching out to different people to benefit from diverse perspectives? Given the extent to which people acquire information and learn how to do their work from other people, these are important considerations in assessing the effectiveness of one's own network.

Giving employees a closer look at their personal networks can help them uncover all kinds of weaknesses. For example, let's return to the network analysis of senior executives in the Americas division of a major technology company. In addition to assessing the effectiveness of the group as we described in chapter 2, we analyzed the personal networks of each of the top leaders. This kind of assessment is often important with senior executives because a significant part of their jobs is to make effective decisions, and most of the information they rely on comes from their networks. Let's consider two of those executives: Neil and Dave, both of whom had significant responsibilities throughout the division.

Dave's network was smaller than Neil's in terms of the number of people seeking information from him (ten people for Dave, fourteen for Neil) as well as the number of people he sought out for information (fourteen people for Dave, twenty-one for Neil). But the difference in network size was not as revealing as the difference in composition. Dave tended to acquire information almost exclusively from those in his functional area; of his ten informal contacts, nine were from his department. By contrast, eight of Neil's fourteen informal contacts were members of his department, and six worked in different functional areas. Other aspects of Dave's network also suggested rigidity. For example, he tended to turn only to people he had known for a long time or had met because they were structured into his schedule. As a result, it was likely that Dave had much less exposure to new concepts and information than Neil—and our interviews with Dave confirmed this. Through his own initiative, and with the help of a coaching program established by senior management, Dave set out to identify and nurture the relationships in which he had underinvested and to decrease his reliance on relationships in which he had overinvested.

Biases in Personal Networks

There are many ways to assess the composition of your network and its impact on what you will learn over time. For example, sociologists commonly look at the effect of certain similarities between people— such as age, race, education, and gender—on clustering in networks. Reflecting on the list of people important to us from an informational or learning point of view often reveals the homogeneity of our networks. Unless we are forced to interact with people different from ourselves, there is an extremely strong tendency, known as homophily, for us to seek out those who are similar.[4] This tendency has a striking effect on what we learn and the views we come to hold.

But this profile does not always illustrate the subtle means by which the people in our network affect our learning. In many coaching sessions with managers at all levels in organizations, we have found at least six dimensions of personal networks to be important on this front.[5]

- *Relative Hierarchical Position.* Networks can be biased by an overreliance on people who occupy certain hierarchical positions. Managing relationships with those higher than, at the same level, and lower than you is a hallmark of a well-rounded social network. Connections with those above you in the hierarchy can be critical for making decisions, acquiring resources, developing political capital, and being aware of events or resources in an organization that are beyond your immediate purview. People at the same level are generally the best for brainstorming and providing specific help or information based on similar work they are doing. Those beneath you are often the best source of technical information and expertise. In general, balance is important, and people's networks seem to fall out of balance when they don't maintain enough relationships overall, when they focus too heavily on those higher in the organization, or when they miss the technical expertise that can often be gained from those at lower levels.

- *Relative Organizational Position.* People tend to pay attention to, interact with, and learn from those in their home department. Hiring, orientation, training, evaluation, and compensation all tend to promote interaction within, and not across, departmental boundaries. Combine this with certain leadership styles, cultural values, and unit-level performance metrics, and it is little wonder that people tend to have few relationships with those in other organizations or in other departments in their own organization. As we move up in the hierarchy, such bridging relationships become increasingly important to ensure effective learning and decision making. Yet when people need such relationships the most, they often have the least time to spend building them.

- *Physical Proximity.* The likelihood of collaborating with someone decreases the farther you are from that person. Distances of only a few feet, let alone floors in a building or even buildings themselves, often prove to be critical fragmentation points in networks. Although collaborative tools such as e-mail, instant messaging, and video conferencing can bridge such gaps, proximity often dictates people's networks. With executives, this problem often results in their not understanding the needs of those in different locations, such as field sites. As a result of their isolation, these executives often make poor decisions.

- *Structure of Interactions.* Does your network promote serendipitous learning and innovation? Look at almost any manager's Day-Timer or Palm Pilot: It is common to see back-to-back meetings from 7 A.M. to 7 P.M. or beyond, day after day. The critical question from a learning perspective is whether the people you are seeking as your primary information conduits are the best sources for the task-relevant information you need, or whether they are simply built into your schedule. We have heard many executives recount poor strategic decisions they made that met nothing but heated resistance—all as a result of not getting the right information from the right parts of the organization. Often, the culprit was a schedule that permitted only certain voices to be heard.

- *Time Invested in Maintaining Relationships.* Do you invest enough time in maintaining relationships that are important to you? People often spend the most time and effort maintaining relationships that need little investment or that are antagonistic and offer little benefit. We all have finite time and energy to put into relationships. Managing these investments wisely can yield substantial performance and learning benefits.

- *Length of Time Known.* Finally, is there diversity in your network in terms of the length of time that you have known people? Again, we believe that balance is best here. If you have known too many people for too long, you are probably hearing things you already know or, more insidious, knowingly or unknowingly using other people to get your own opinions confirmed. It is good to see new people cycling into (and out of) a person's network as his or her job changes. At the same time, if you have too many new people in your network, it may indicate a lack of sounding boards or confidants with whom you can discuss personal or inflammatory issues.

Combining these dimensions to assess your personal network can give you insight about where to focus your relationship building. For example, consider two executives, each of whom listed fifteen people in his personal network. A close look at the profiles of these networks reveals striking differences.

Figure 5-4 shows the network of a senior executive in a major electronics organization. Having recently been promoted to this position, he found that most of the people he relied on at this point were new to him. Although he was pleased with this network from an informational perspective, he was less comfortable with the extent to which he could trust these people to discuss and brainstorm tough organizational issues. One implication of this assessment was a need to rekindle relationships with two past mentors who could be distant advisers.

Additional biases existed. For example, he was concerned about his excessive reliance on people lower in the hierarchy and on those in his

FIGURE 5-4

Lack of Relationships Reaching Up in the Organization

Network Size: 15

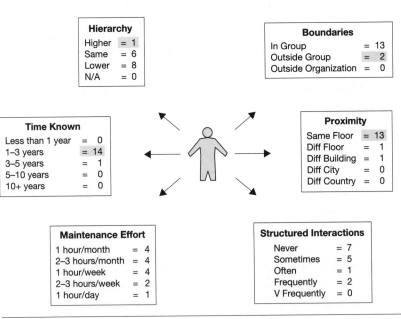

own group. He had set out to build relationships with his employees in order to be an effective leader, but it was clear to him that he had not established sufficient relationships with those higher in the organization. As a result, he often missed opportunities to leverage resources or knowledge that existed elsewhere in the organization, and he was less able to gain buy-in on initiatives he wanted to pursue. He was also surprised to note his heavy reliance on those physically near him. The network analysis showed him that two practices—relying too heavily on spontaneity and failing to systematically reach out to those in different locations—were biasing the information he had to work from. To fix this imbalance, he began to structure time into his calendar for people he might not necessarily bump into in the halls or cafeteria.

Now consider figure 5-5, a profile of a government executive brought in to manage a critical division of an agency. This man was relatively new in his role and had spent a great deal of time his first year meeting

FIGURE 5-5

Overreliance on People from the Same Group

Network Size: 15

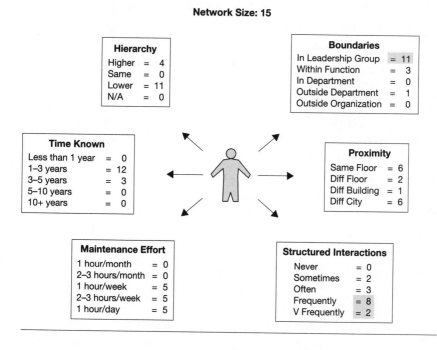

Hierarchy	
Higher	= 4
Same	= 0
Lower	= 11
N/A	= 0

Boundaries	
In Leadership Group	= 11
Within Function	= 3
In Department	= 0
Outside Department	= 1
Outside Organization	= 0

Time Known	
Less than 1 year	= 0
1–3 years	= 12
3–5 years	= 3
5–10 years	= 0
10+ years	= 0

Proximity	
Same Floor	= 6
Diff Floor	= 2
Diff Building	= 1
Diff City	= 6

Maintenance Effort	
1 hour/month	= 0
2–3 hours/month	= 0
1 hour/week	= 5
2–3 hours/week	= 5
1 hour/day	= 5

Structured Interactions	
Never	= 0
Sometimes	= 2
Often	= 3
Frequently	= 8
V Frequently	= 2

and establishing shared goals with his extended leadership team. The concern here, in his eyes, was an excessive reliance on this group of people. Although he was turning to those higher in the agency, the remainder of his informational relationships tended to come from his leadership team. A critical step for him was to develop two kinds of relationships: those deeper within the agency to get a ground-level view of events, and those outside the agency to ensure fresh perspectives. He was also concerned about his heavy reliance on people who were built into his schedule. After reviewing his overloaded schedule, he quickly noted that the amount of time he spent with the same people led to comfortable relationships but likely did nothing to help him develop new insights or perspectives.

Expertise Gaps

In addition to relational composition, we push executives to consider their *expertise network* (detailed in appendix B). Many managers turn to others with specific expertise every day. If you have a gap in your expertise network, you are left with no one to turn to and should look for means of filling this gap. You also want to avoid being overly reliant on a small number of people. What happens if a person you turn to regularly moves to a different department or leaves the organization? Can you immediately locate someone to fill that gap?

A colleague of ours in a small research group found that he had become too reliant on a small group of people. He had worked with them closely for several years, and he very much depended on four of them for help and advice. After a staff realignment following a merger, he found that two of the people in his network had moved to a different organization and the other two had been transferred to different departments in a different city. Although these people were still accessible to him, after about six months our colleague realized that his go-to people no longer had the up-to-date expertise he required. This overreliance on former coworkers had left our colleague with a large expertise gap. Although he was eventually able to seek out new people within his group, his dislike of change had hampered his short-term effectiveness.

Similarly, in a software company we worked with, one of the programmers had recently moved to a different division. He quickly realized that although his old network provided him with go-to people for some of the expertise he needed, he now needed to develop expertise in new areas. Because this role was complex he could not master every aspect of the work, and he found he needed to foster new connections quickly. This is a common situation for people who have changed positions. The key is first to be aware that you have an expertise gap and then to use existing contacts to help fill it. A substantial part of the personal network diagnostic outlined in appendix B focuses on helping people to identify and address (or prepare for the potential of) expertise gaps.

A Bird's-Eye View

Managers can take substantial and targeted action to promote connectivity by working with individuals in networks. When viewing a full network diagram, managers can identify four key roles—central connectors, boundary spanners, information brokers, and peripheral members—and use that information to efficiently promote appropriate connectivity. Perhaps even more important, managers can provide employees with diagnostic information that they can use to develop their own personal networks. This grassroots approach can be an efficient means of promoting connectivity both inside and outside an organization.

Appendix B outlines a simple personal network diagnostic, and we encourage you to take a few moments to apply this perspective to your own network. Such assessments can help people learn and develop professionally and can also be a critical way to develop rich, vibrant networks within an entire organization. Several organizations we have worked with are implementing this diagnostic approach in career-development processes. In these settings, annual development goals include *both* content-related learning and network development objectives. Structuring this kind of development process into the work of an entire organization can have dramatic effects on the connectivity of strategically important groups.

Individuals in a network are always our first focus and prove to be a good place for managers to start looking for ways to improve collaboration and connectivity. Managers can also improve connectivity through efforts to build relationships within the network. This requires them to attend to the stage of development of most of the relationships within the network. The next chapter shows managers what actions have the most effect on relationships in a network, as well as how effective management of these relationships changes over time.

6

Building Bridges

Initiating, Developing, and Maintaining Networks

I think it is helpful to think of where relationships are in terms of cycles or development. My leadership team has pulsated over the fifteen years that I have been in charge. When employee participation was the rage, the "team" grew quite large, really a committee at one point, so that everyone had a say. In retrospect I am not sure I really worked with those people well, mostly because I didn't know what they knew or what to rely on them for. Even in that larger team context I still only listened to certain people I trusted. Now the team is back to a more manageable size, and we know each other's strengths and weaknesses, but my guess is that we are locked into another set of problems in that we don't change our minds about what others can be good at and have opinions on. So in addition to network position, I think we need to consider development of relations, maybe a norming, storming, forming view of networks.

—CEO of a financial services organization

Off-site gatherings, strategic planning retreats, all-hands meetings, and brown-bag lunches are rich forums for improving connectivity. In either face-to-face or virtual formats, you can build relationships by presenting network results to a group and then using subgroups to discuss and report back on opportunities for improvement. This is particularly true when you form the subgroups with an eye to mending an important disconnect in the network.

For example, a consumer products company held an off-site session to work on the problem of rigid functional boundaries. Attendees divided into six cross-functional subgroups and generated solutions to problems ranging from network insularity to lack of energy. At a different off-site meeting for a professional services firm whose network closely mirrored formal reporting relationships, cross-hierarchy groups created action plans to address twelve problem points. These solutions became part of a calendar, and over the next year specific steps were taken each month to improve network connectivity.

We can't overemphasize the power of these full-group sessions. Even the most recalcitrant and removed people in the room quickly begin to engage in discussions when network maps and results are presented. In this book we have shared diagrams of people you do not know in companies we have had to disguise. Imagine your own level of interest if you were considering a network of yourself and your colleagues. This becomes particularly engaging when we project from a laptop and so are able to assess various scenarios with the group by shifting employees around in the network, building in relationships that are needed or considering the network effect if certain people or relationships are lost.

However, as the CEO quoted earlier suggests, these sessions can be even more effective when a network's general stage of development is taken into account. People who are new to each other, as in a merger or restructuring, will benefit from different kinds of relationship-building initiatives than will established networks in which relationships have become entrenched, perhaps in unproductive patterns.

To develop more precise means of promoting connectivity, we interviewed forty managers, asking them to describe the history of relationships with three people they had come to rely on for information. Through these interviews, we identified three important phases that relationships often move through, which we call initiation, development, and maintenance/correction. We discuss each phase here, and appendix B includes two facilitation exercises that are useful for each stage of development.

Initiating Relationships

The first challenge in restructurings, mergers, or other initiatives that bring employees together is simply to introduce newfound colleagues in a productive way. The problem is that most team-building exercises are concerned with process issues. This focus may help create a harmonious environment, but it does little to educate team members about each other's skills and abilities. When people come together to engage in a task, they tend to talk about something they all have in common instead of what may be unique about various members of the group. Of course, finding shared interests, acquaintances, and experiences helps us start conversations with people we do not know. But the result is that group members often experience what is called the unshared knowledge problem.[1] They do not learn about their teammates' unique skills and abilities until late in the project (if at all).

Creating an awareness of group members' expertise, as outlined in chapter 3, is only the first relationship-building challenge in newly formed groups; the second is to help people envision how their expertise can be jointly applied. It does a technologist little good, for example, to know that a new colleague has deep skills in process improvement methodologies unless the technologist also understands how those skills complement his or her own. Building this awareness is critical to collaboration in newly formed groups.

We assessed the information flow network of an internal consulting practice formed to provide services to a global bank. This group was the product of a restructuring effort to unite employees who had deep expertise in process improvement, organizational development and change, and technical applications. Leadership believed that integrating these groups would allow them to improve core processes throughout the bank by attending simultaneously to people, process, and technology issues.

But the information flow network revealed a problem. Even though people from the three areas had been brought together into one practice, collaboration was not occurring between the groups. This was not the result of practice members' being unaware of each other's expertise: A review of the awareness network revealed that it was five times better connected across subgroups than the information flow network. For some reason, though, employees were not acting on their knowledge. Sometimes this can be a product of misaligned organizational design or other aspects of organizational context such as leadership behavior or cultural values (which we discuss in chapter 7). We interviewed participants in this network and found that context was not the issue. Rather, employees suggested that the problem was that they had little understanding of *how* their expertise should be combined on projects as well as *why* they should invest the time and effort to make this happen.

The bank's management decided to bring the division together at a half-day off-site meeting. After an hour-long presentation on the results of the network analysis and a question and answer period, participants broke into smaller groups to suggest opportunities for improvement. Many sound recommendations emerged, but the most dramatic outcome occurred at the end of the session, when managers defined in a series of PowerPoint slides what they considered the ideal project. In this fictional internal consulting example, seamless integration of the skills in the process, technology, and organizational-development subgroups resulted in dramatic performance improvements for the bank. After this description, the managers then talked through a timeline for this ideal project, from selling an internal customer to project completion, and they sketched the timeline on butcher block paper tacked to a wall.

Employees were then organized into cross-functional groups and asked to define where different kinds of expertise could be brought to bear throughout the project. The ensuing discussion began to create awareness not only of whose skills and expertise fit where but also why and how such skills should be integrated. Of course, in reality this ideal project would never exist. But it helped employees see, in a pragmatic way, how better collaboration could improve their work. Employees also walked away with a newfound understanding of some of their colleagues' expertise as well as how it fit with their own.

Defining an ideal project is particularly effective for forming relationships when you're dealing with mergers or large-scale change efforts or you're launching large groups focused on a specific output, such as new-product development teams or alliances. The technique rapidly builds awareness of expertise in the network as well as an understanding of when and why to leverage newfound colleagues.

Developing Professional and Personal Relationships

Understanding how dimensions of relationships develop over time can help move networks from simple contacts to important conduits of information. Our interviewees suggested that relationships considered critical for information developed along two tracks: the professional and the personal. As relationships progress on both fronts, interpersonal trust is built and improves the quality of collaboration.

Professional Development

People strengthen their relationships on a professional front as they gain a more precise awareness of others' skills and expertise. This calibration yields a finer grained understanding of the kinds of information we seek from specific people and thus increases the success of interactions over time.

However, developing a deeper understanding of others' knowledge and skills is only one part of building a collaborative relationship. Another important dimension is learning how to gain access to these people. Some people are quick to respond to e-mail, others to voice mail, and still others prefer face-to-face interaction. The people we interviewed said that they developed an awareness of how best to connect with a given person, often after some initial missteps. We heard stories of people becoming increasingly frustrated—and almost deciding to give up—after leaving a series of voice mails with no response, only to learn that a single e-mail was returned promptly. We also heard people describe experts who did not respond to e-mail but in a face-to-face interaction were generous with both time and ideas.

Beyond media, though, the way we make requests of others also affects the likelihood of a timely response and is a crucial part of developing a collaborative relationship. We asked interviewees whether they approach specific people in their network with a personal appeal—for example, saying that they are in a bind and need information quickly—or with a professional appeal that highlights the benefits for the other person. Interestingly, the response time for personal appeals was literally half that for professional appeals. But, of course, personal appeals usually succeed only if the parties have a personal relationship. You can't reach out to just anyone, say "I need help," and expect to get it.

Personal Development

If anything surprised us from our interviews, it was the importance of relationships developing on a personal front to become effective professionally (in terms of information sharing and collaboration). Almost universally, people reported that their most valued information relationships had connected on issues outside work, and this process was often identified as a major milestone in the development of the relationship. Despite numerous technical mediums of contact, the social aspect of a relationship often determined whether someone would respond in a timely fashion. It also seemed to affect the extent to which a person learned from another.

Managers can help employees forge productive workplace relationships by creating opportunities for people to connect on non-work-related matters. A crucial component of the facilitation exercises in appendix B or technologies such as expertise locators is making some non-work-related information available to others. To be sure, managers want to respect people's privacy and not be invasive, but revealing the kind of information we are describing has not been a problem in the organizations we have worked with.

Although it seems simple, one of the most productive devices we have employed has been a *persona book* or baseball-type cards that introduce people on both a personal and professional front (see figure 6-1). The medium is not the key here; the information can be put online or distributed on paper. Rather, the key to making these devices useful is

FIGURE 6-1

Persona Book Template

to include personal information. Adding hobbies, educational backgrounds, or answers to idiosyncratic questions such as "Who would you most like to be stuck in an elevator with?" makes new colleagues human and approachable.

When we conduct follow-up network assessments with such groups, we ask people what helped them deepen relationships within the network. They immediately say that personal information about another person was important. Of course they also looked at a person's professional background and expertise before seeking them out, but the personal information was critical to the decision to reach out. It also usually provided the basis for starting a conversation with a stranger.

Does Trust Really Matter?

Developing relationships on professional and personal fronts helps generate trust.[2] Interpersonal trust is elusive, however, and it is not clearly tied to the informational and learning effectiveness of relationships. One skeptical senior manager told us, "I think all the recent attention on social capital and trust is off the mark. People go where they need to, to get information, regardless of whether they trust or like someone. I may not like or trust [someone he recently turned to], but if I need to know something I am going to go ask him. My world moves too fast not to do this." Before suggesting that managers should develop trust to promote collaboration in networks, we set out to discover whether it really mattered.

We first sought to determine whether trust affected information seeking by assessing trust in networks with several organizations. For example, we conducted a social network analysis of the entire staff of caregivers and administrators in a health clinic. This organization was designed functionally with the intent that three caregiving departments seamlessly provide therapeutic treatment to patients with a given need. We assessed a series of information and trust relationships and used the chart in figure 6-2 to help pinpoint critical disconnects in the trust network within and between departments.

Looking down the diagonal, we find a fairly high level of trusting relationships within each department. In fact, these percentages would have been higher except that they included people who worked different shifts within a unit and so had never met one another. However, when we move off the diagonal we see some potentially important disconnects between departments. Here we find a substantial lack of

FIGURE 6-2

Trust in a Mental Health Clinic

	Caregiving Unit 1	Caregiving Unit 2	Caregiving Unit 3	Administration
Caregiving Unit 1	49%			
Caregiving Unit 2	8%	56%		
Caregiving Unit 3	32%	44%	64%	
Administration	5%	9%	7%	59%

trust between administration and the three caregiving units, resulting in an us/them mentality.

We also find a low level of trust between caregiving units 1 and 2. Despite needing to collaborate to provide effective patient care, people within these two units often were not willing to ask each other for or share information, for two reasons. First, asking a colleague from the other department was considered embarrassing and a threat to self-esteem. Rather than being productive encounters for the patient, these interactions were often ones where care providers postured to try and make the other care provider look ignorant or incompetent in his or her job. Second, people were concerned about their reputation and worried that a specific interaction might be distorted to make them look bad and then circulated through the grapevine. One care provider put it this way: "I wouldn't go there. First it's a pride thing. I don't want to look like I am groveling. And I don't want my boss to know, either, as she always makes fun of them. But I am sure this affects what the [patients] get here. I mean the whole way we are organized is with the intent that the [primary caregiving units] integrate across lines as needed by the patient, but there is clearly a lack of trust across that line that critically affects working together and patient treatment."

Ten Actions for Building Trust in Relationships

Given the potential implications of trust in networks, we engaged in a separate phase of research at the Institute for Knowledge-Based Organizations. Working with Daniel Levin of Rutgers University, we surveyed people in three global companies in different countries to assess statistically the importance of interpersonal trust for learning and information flow.[3]

We found that two types of trust play a significant role in how effectively people learn from each other. The first is *competence-based trust*, which focuses on ability: I believe that you know what you are talking about; I am willing to allow you to shape my thinking. When we trust people in this way, we are likely to listen to them and believe what they say; we trust their competence. This form of trust accrues within a group as members have opportunities to become aware of and develop a detailed understanding of other people's expertise.

The second is *benevolence-based trust*—what most of us mean when we talk about trust. It focuses on vulnerability: I trust that you will not think poorly of me or tell others if I don't know much about a given topic. Trusting someone's benevolence allows us to expose our lack of knowledge and ask the questions we need answered. When people have this kind of trust, they are more forthright about their true expertise and much more likely to be creative, learning what they need to so that they can do something better or differently.

The survey phase of our research gave us confidence that trust is important to effective knowledge transfer. To provide practical ideas to managers about how to promote interpersonal trust, we conducted interviews across twenty organizations.[4] From this we developed ten actions for promoting interpersonal trust that are important for leaders to model and reward as well as to embed in human resource practices. Let's look at each in detail.

Act with Discretion

When someone requests that certain information be kept confidential, doing otherwise violates the person's trust.[5] The need to keep confidences is particularly important in information seeking, because the most useful advice often comes from a back-and-forth sharing of all potentially relevant information. If people feel it is not safe to reveal such information, they may withhold facts that could help solve the problem, or information seekers may not be honest about the extent of their own ignorance. Our interviewees indicated that people who kept sensitive material to themselves were perceived as more trustworthy.

Though a seemingly obvious prescription, acting with discretion was far from common. In fact, our interviewees frequently described using people's lack of discretion intentionally as a means of circulating information within a network. This creates a problem when everyone believes that what is discussed will likely be shared—even though assurances of confidentiality have been made. Willingness to be open and vulnerable in asking for help rapidly diminishes throughout a group. Managers have an ability to promote discretion both through their own actions and by holding others accountable for this behavior.

Match Words and Deeds

Consistency between word and deed is an important determinant of trust because it allows people to place credence in what we say rather than try to determine ulterior motives or hidden agendas.[6] Almost any member of an organization will tell you that people who "walk the talk" are more trusted. If a person often tells you one thing but then does another, it is only natural to wonder whether he or she really cares about you or your interests when giving you advice.

There are two challenges here. First, you must be aware of and act consistently with the implicit and explicit commitments we all make many times over in a day. Small differences in expectations between two people can cause substantial problems in trust over time. Second, setting realistic expectations is equally important. People who are more trusted tend to set realistic expectations of what they can accomplish and then almost always deliver on their commitments. A well-intentioned tendency to overcommit can be dangerous to credibility over time.

Communicate Often and Well

Frequent communication increases the amount of information available to help one person assess another's abilities, intentions, and behaviors within the relationship.[7] Rich media, such as face-to-face interactions, give you greater ability to connect with another person and provide more opportunity for people to develop a shared vision and language.

Establish a Shared Vision and Language

Some have suggested that a shared vision and shared language promote trust in networks.[8] Establishing common goals and terminology can be particularly important at the start of a project. For example, one manager we interviewed described a new-product development team that had decided *not* to spend time ensuring that team members shared terminology and expectations. Unfortunately, fissures in the group appeared early, and within one or two months the situation had deteriorated to the point of crisis.

First, group members interpreted the team's mandate differently. Everyone thought they were doing appropriate work, but when they met to review progress, people had gone in different directions seemingly without reason. The team members were unaware that they were interpreting the team's directions differently. They thought that their coworkers were doing bad work or, worse, were pursuing political agendas.

Second, in terms of shared language, the same words occasionally meant different things to different people. In one almost comical situation, a significant lack of trust developed between two team members—one from the United States and one from England—based on different meanings attached to the word *quite*. To the U.S. team member, *quite* was a modifier meaning "a lot of something"—so saying the new software was quite effective at a given application meant that it was very effective. In contrast, for the English teammate, saying an application of the software was quite effective meant that this part of the program was just getting by, that it was not all that effective. Over time, hearing each other use that one word differently in discussions with customers, superiors, and other team members led each to believe that the other person was posturing. This created a great deal of mistrust in terms of both competence ("Is he blind? How could he say that was 'quite' effective?") and benevolence ("He is trying to make his part of this project look better in the eyes of an important manager!") until, at a cocktail party, one of them serendipitously learned the different meanings attached to this word. Of course, this same kind of misinterpretation occurs frequently as people from different functional, educational, or cultural backgrounds attach unique meanings to similar words or phrases.

Highlight Knowledge Domain Boundaries

As outlined earlier, determining what another person knows is a challenge when interactions have been limited or the seeker does not know much about the knowledge domain. Although demonstrations of competence are an important signal of trustworthiness, knowledge sources suggest that they can be trusted when they clarify what they *do not* know. In many organizations, the pressure to be an expert in all areas drives people to answer questions with more confidence than they should. It became clear in our interviews, however, that defining the limits of one's expertise markedly distinguishes trusted sources from less trusted ones.

Know When to Step Out of Your Role

People occupy roles at work that dictate how they "should" act.[9] These expectations can create barriers that make it impossible for trust to grow. Almost all our interviewees said that breaking down those barriers and establishing a personal connection was crucial for a productive relationship. Discovering non–work-related commonalities—such as education, family status, management philosophies, and political leanings—helped them feel that they related to each other on more than an instrumental basis. Of course, the extent to which people are willing to disclose personal details depends on their individual comfort level. But establishing a non–work-related connection seems to pay dividends in promoting interpersonal trust.

Give Away Something of Value

Giving without expecting something in return is a show of trust. In such situations, the giver takes initial action based on a belief that the receiver will respond in kind at some future point.[10] In our interviews it was clear that knowledge seekers often looked for such signals to determine how much they could trust someone's benevolence. When someone provided access to a limited or sensitive resource, information seekers often took it as a sign that the person viewed them as trustworthy. This, in turn, often promoted reciprocal trust in the person sought for information.

Two primary examples of these limited or sensitive resources emerged in the interviews. First, sharing tacit, or experiential, knowledge often led to the development of benevolence-based trust. Describing the subtleties and nuances of managing a sensitive account, or dealing with a difficult supervisor, can expose people who serve as knowledge sources on a number of levels. Not only are they investing time to share their knowledge, but they are also revealing knowledge that leaves them open to second-guessing about their past decisions. Sharing personal contacts is a second important type of assistance. Revealing one's personal contacts can jeopardize reputation and social capital. Allowing outsiders to tap into one's network is a signal of trust that a person will often respect and reciprocate.

Help People Refine Unclear Ideas

Many important situations in organizations are inherently ambiguous, where problem resolution requires framing to make sure that the right problem is being solved. However, the spoken or unspoken norm of many leaders in Corporate America is: "Come to me with solutions, not problems." Welcoming exploration and potentially ill-formed thoughts and solutions at appropriate junctures can be critical to the development of trust in a relationship. In many situations, people who are seeking information are not completely sure of the question they are asking, let alone the answer. People who encourage inquiry in problem solving are viewed as more trustworthy than those who don't tolerate ambiguity or exploration.

Make Decisions Fair and Transparent

Although our interviews emphasized the relationship between an information seeker and a source, we also found that trust in management "trickled down" to influence trust between employees. At issue are both fairness (applying rules equally to individuals) and transparency (revealing how and why rules are applied). The extent to which management was able to incorporate fairness and transparency into decision-making processes played a role in how people viewed their relationships with others in the organization.

For example, many of our interviewees complained that the standards for promotions and rewards were not always clear and did not seem to be applied equally. This lack of equity, or at least transparency, in decisions influenced the general perception of trustworthiness across a range of topics and colleagues. One interviewee critiqued his organization's promotion system, indicating that mistrust led to "an inbred organization" and cast suspicion on all the reward systems. In fact, throughout the interviews, promotions and promotion standards were one of the hot buttons, along with career path, salary, and evaluations. When these were viewed as unfair, employees began to perceive even inconsequential comments with suspicion. Rather than trusting someone's word, facts, or opinion, people felt that they had to check and double-check what was said. Furthermore, by playing cards close to the chest, employees did not engage in discussions or put forth ideas that might not be considered absolutely correct for fear of the consequences.

Hold People Accountable for Trustworthy Behavior

The well-known mantra that you get what you reinforce and reward can be applied to trust.[11] Several of the organizations we observed were evaluating and recognizing trust as demonstrated by employees' behaviors. One interviewee noted that his company clearly articulated the importance of trust in its values. The company was willing to spend time and energy to train everyone in the importance of these values and to work out a comprehensive evaluation process assessing employees' behavior in relation to these values. Many companies may say that they value integrity, but not as many will put their employees through training, and few of those will formulate a working evaluation system and tie in compensation. This organization did all those things. As a result, employees held themselves and each other accountable to the stated values, and in this way they became organizational norms.

Tangible rewards—not stiff penalties—also encourage trustworthy behavior. In our interviews we heard about several types of evaluation systems addressing trust. In one organization, managers wrote paragraphs about various aspects of an employee's performance and rated employees on trust-related dimensions. In another firm, trust was measured as part of a quantitative assessment. Trust and associated behavior constituted one of six areas on the evaluation form that managers completed for their direct reports. Although not everyone weighted it as one-sixth of the evaluation (some thought it more important, others less), everyone thought it significant that trust was mentioned explicitly. In both organizations, people felt that management's effort to recognize demonstrated trustworthiness had a profound effect on the development of interpersonal trust.

Correcting Unproductive Behaviors

Organizations can do all the right things to help people initiate and develop networks but, as relationships grow, unproductive patterns can develop and over time become entrenched. Network analysis can be helpful in these situations. Trying to correct a single person's disruptive influence on a group can invoke defensiveness; offenders can be quick to claim that the problem is not their doing. Such defensiveness from someone high in the organization is even harder to deal with. Confronting powerful people can be difficult without real evidence that certain behaviors are a problem. Network analysis provides that evidence.

Avoiding Network Lock-in

When certain people become overloaded—something that happens most often when networks rely too heavily on experts or formal leaders—the entire network becomes locked into a damaging pattern. The problem is that overly central people try so hard to get their work done that they cannot step back and consider inefficiencies in the way they are working. They have little time to determine why and take corrective action. As described in chapter 5, network analysis can make this problem visible, and managers can correct it by reallocating tasks, information domains, and decision rights.

Lock-in occurs on the relationship level as well. One of the most surprising discoveries in our interviews was that many productive relationships begin with poor first impressions that change over time when people have no choice but to work together. In general, though, our results suggest that people learn the most about their colleagues in the first twelve months. After that, they increasingly turn to a limited set of established contacts they have come to trust, even when other people might have superior expertise.

To some degree this is efficient, but it can create blind spots if we continually return to the same people. Worse, we tend to narrowly define what we allow trusted advisers to be good at, sometimes missing expertise they have developed since we last spoke with them. This may resonate with your experience. Have you ever been surprised by a colleague's expertise that you were unaware of? Because we are too busy and cynical, or overly dependent on stereotypes, we are quick to label what we think others can be good at and often do not discover and benefit from their actual expertise.

This means that groups often need structured ways of updating awareness of the expertise of others. We conducted a network analysis of a recently formed department in a technology organization. In the beginning of this project the entire group had met and engaged in activities designed to help people become aware of the knowledge and skills of others. This meeting was followed by a second one four months later. In addition, monthly conference calls were initiated. During each call a person from one of the projects was nominated to update the group on the project. This communicated to everyone the knowledge and expertise that resided in the group. It is crucial to structure these experiences in ways that almost force people to listen. Unfortunately, we tend to believe that if we know someone, we also know that person's skills and abilities—a belief that can be far from the truth.

Political Tensions

Sometimes sparse or fragmented networks are the result of political motives or ambitions. When two leaders disagree or are posturing, the fissure between them radiates down into the network and can quickly create tightly clustered groups and an us/them mentality. We conducted a social network analysis of the innovation management practice of a large consulting firm. To compete more effectively with other consulting firms, this firm was going through a significant restructuring designed to combine the expertise of several groups into one practice. To better understand this network, the partner leading the practice invited us to conduct a network analysis.

We immediately noticed significant clustering in three tightly knit subgroups: two in North America and one in Europe. A series of changes was undertaken that we have described elsewhere,[12] but for our purposes here we want to highlight the challenge created by the groups in the United States. It turned out that most of the people in these two groups had offices not only in the same building but also along the same corridor. Physical proximity, then, was not an issue. Rather, our interviews revealed a political problem between the two partners in charge of each subgroup. These partners were polar opposites in personality as well as in their approach to the business. Although the partner leading the practice had an inkling of the problem, the visual representation of the network diagram clearly showed the extent to which this interpersonal tension radiated down in the network and affected performance of the overall group.

Various steps were taken to help resolve the problem. For example, an executive coach was brought in to help the two partners talk through their differences and develop plans to improve their approach to conflict. The coaching helped them turn what had become a rivalry into a strength as they found ways to appreciate and leverage each other's abilities. And they took things one step further by airing, lightheartedly, parts of their discussions at an all-hands meeting so that their employees helped hold them accountable to each other.

Redundant Relationships

Another productivity drain we see in networks is excessive connectivity. All of us likely have been dragged into meetings we didn't truly need to attend. Consensus is a good thing, but excessive concern with involving everyone in decisions and not taking action until total consensus has been reached can kill momentum. This was clearly the case in a software company we assessed. Although it was the most connected group we have seen, no one was able to get work done because of the sheer volume of meetings, calls, e-mails, and instant messages. Rather than build connectivity, the focus of this assessment was to shed some relationships and provide clarity on decision rights and accountabilities so that decision making would not be cumbersome.

When you work with teams within broader networks (such as top leadership teams, new-product development teams, or permanent work teams), it is also worth considering whether team members are maintaining too many of the same relationships. For example, we worked closely with coleaders of a government agency whose networks, we discovered, were almost identical (see figures 6-3a and 6-3b). Interviews showed that the two managers were not accomplishing as much as they could if they were more diversified and better leveraged each other's networks. In addition, there were bottlenecks within the network because they both attended many of the same meetings. Scheduling is hard enough with one boss and can become nearly impossible with two. Moreover, they were largely hearing the same information. Rather than bouncing ideas off of each other and getting different viewpoints, they trafficked in such similar information environments that they got little from each other's viewpoints except validation of their own thinking. A detailed personal network assessment (as outlined in appendix B)

FIGURE 6-3a

Redundant Leadership Networks: Leader 1

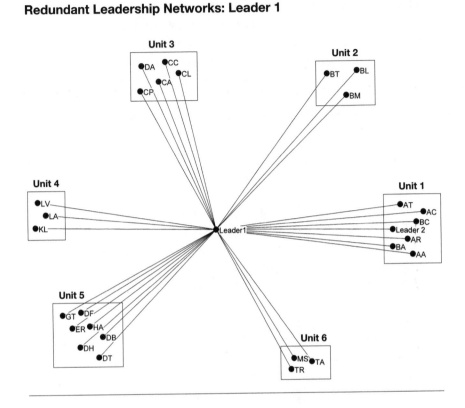

helped them reconsider *as a team* the relationships that each should focus on to be more efficient.

Making the Connection

Rather than general-purpose team-building activities, we have used our research to develop customized exercises to nurture effective information relationships where it matters most in the organization. Of course, even the most carefully developed changes will be short-lived if the organizational context does not support new patterns of collaboration. Aspects of organizational design—such as formal structure, performance- and work-management processes, and human resource

FIGURE 6-3b

Redundant Leadership Networks: Leader 2

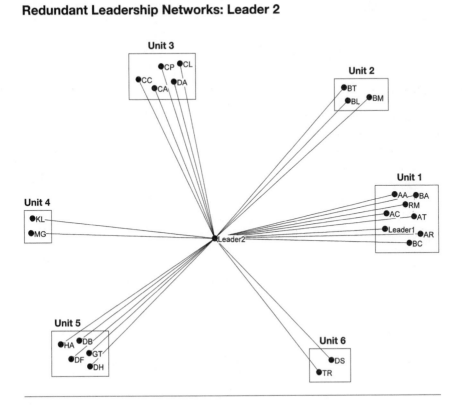

practices—can have striking effects on network connectivity. Similarly, softer aspects, such as leadership and organizational culture, can also throw networks into unproductive patterns. Considering these elements is a critical part of sustaining appropriate network connectivity, and is the challenge we turn to next.

7

Breaking the Mold

Aligning Organizational Context to Support Social Networks

The strength of the network analysis is that it gives you a visual of what's going on and allows you to make specific adjustments. But you also really have to pay attention to aspects of the organization that affect collaboration. Networks don't exist in a vacuum. Things like culture, incentives, leadership, and hierarchy influence who speaks to whom. I think what our maps show is that if you just try to intervene inside the network and ignore organizational forces that are kind of pressing on the network in various ways, you are fighting a losing battle and likely to see things snap back to unproductive patterns. Not only is this a waste of time, but it will lead to cynicism for future efforts.

—Managing partner of a technology consulting organization

A CONSULTING FIRM we worked with had invested substantially in changing its structure from one with an office in each major city, each with profit and loss responsibility, to one that consolidated these offices into four regions throughout the United States. Most of the firm's competitors had moved to national or global practices and were often able to assemble a team of more qualified and skilled consultants for clients than this firm, which drew from local staffing pools. The firm's leaders initiated the reorganization to increase the depth and breadth of expertise that could be applied to client projects and competitive sales situations. They anticipated that the change in structure would not only stem loss of market share but also would increase efficiency, because consultants would not be re-creating solutions developed in other offices.

Eighteen months after the restructuring, we were asked to conduct a series of social network analyses to assess collaboration in the newly formed regions. We mapped several different practices in each of the regions and found that the firm was enjoying mixed success, at best. Consider, for example, two practices in different regions. The first practice was fragmented into three subgroups reflecting the major cities in that region (see figure 7-1). Collaboration was heavily restricted by location, with very few connections between the cities.

In the second region, we mapped a group with almost identical characteristics in terms of size, work, and geographic dispersion. As shown

FIGURE 7-1

Fragmented Consulting Practice

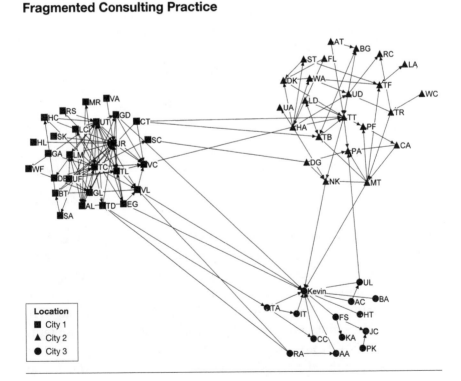

in figure 7-2, here we found a very different pattern of collaboration across the three primary cities in this region. In contrast to the fragmented network of the first region, this group had begun to collaborate and leverage expertise effectively throughout the region to support sales opportunities and client projects.

This was not a trivial issue. With its multimillion-dollar investment, management was betting the future of the firm on an ability to integrate employees' expertise. But some regions were so fragmented that the practices could not deliver high-quality consulting services. Stories abounded in these regions of employees not providing the best solution (or doing so inefficiently) because they were not aware of expertise or project experience that existed in other offices in that region. The more integrated practices had different stories to tell. They were much more likely to have tapped into expertise in other offices in time to make a difference on sales opportunities or projects.

FIGURE 7-2

Integrated Consulting Practice

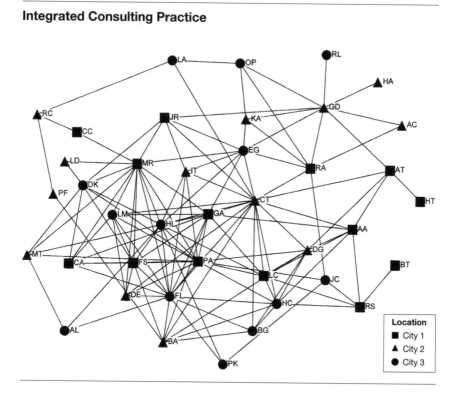

In addition to helping win competitive bids and deliver high-quality solutions, the ability to leverage knowledge and solutions across offices dramatically improved efficiency in client projects.

Clearly, the firm needed to improve connectivity in the fragmented networks, but it was also critical to address aspects of organizational context that encouraged network fragmentation. In this case, we found differences in management that had a strong influence on network integration and the comparative performance of the practices. For example, except for the partners, who had periodic face-to-face meetings, the group in the more fragmented region had no forum for coming together, meeting each other, and learning about colleagues' skills and expertise. But what the fragmented region deemed as an unnecessary expense, the better-connected region considered critical. In the cohesive network, employees indicated that other people in the region became viable sources of information only after they had met face-to-face and had an opportunity to understand one another's strengths. Even though they used a state-of-the-art skill-profiling system, it was the personal, face-to-face contact that dictated whether and how people trusted others enough to reach out to them for information.

Just as important, staffing practices were different in the two groups. Rather than focus exclusively on efficiency and billable hours, the more cohesive group recognized that effective relationships developed during projects. As a result, staffing decisions were often made with an eye to integrating people from different locations, a decision that flies in the face of conventional wisdom. Given the start-up and marketing costs for each project, it is often more efficient to staff one person for six months on a project rather than two people for three months. However, recognizing the importance of relationships from both a morale and a future network perspective, leaders in the more connected network made what might appear to be a poor economic decision in pursuit of a longer-term payoff.

The two groups also employed different human resource practices despite a common, firmwide HR policy and procedure manual. For example, although both groups used a critical-incident interviewing technique, the cohesive group looked for evidence of collaborative behavior in job candidates, whereas the fragmented group was more focused on individual achievements such as sales ability or technical skills. The fragmented group followed the firm's typical two-day new-hire orientation session. The cohesive group supplemented this orientation by posting new hires' pictures and resumes in a heavily traveled hallway, taking them to lunch with a large cross section of the group, and mounting a scavenger hunt that helped new employees find and learn about others in the organization.

In performance evaluation, the fragmented group collected peer feedback but made bonus decisions based only on billable hours and revenue generation. In this way, managers sent a clear signal about what employees should be doing with their time. In contrast, the cohesive group took the peer-feedback process seriously, and it had an effect on advancement and compensation decisions.

We offered a variety of recommendations that improved consistency of collaboration throughout the regions. But, as the senior partner articulated in the quotation at the beginning of this chapter, these recommendations needed to ensure that organizational context supported desired patterns. Throughout our work, we have seen that promoting appropriate collaboration requires ensuring that organizational context does not drive groups back to unproductive patterns. The remainder of this chapter describes important elements of context, and appendix B reflects these ideas in a diagnostic we often include with our network surveys. Executives, by virtue of their privileged position in the hierarchy, often believe that organizational design, culture, and leadership have more positive impacts on collaboration than employees deep in the organization believe. Our diagnostic approach provides important feedback to help alter these misperceptions.

We have touched on some of these ideas in examples earlier in the book. But here we provide a holistic framework of organizational context for managers trying to nurture appropriate network connectivity.[1] Although organizations usually take action on only a handful of issues that significantly affect collaboration, it is important to consider all these dimensions because critical elements of context are not always obvious.

Creating a Collaborative Organizational Context

Of the networks we worked with in our research program, we picked twenty that were either particularly well connected or particularly sparse or fragmented. We then interviewed six to ten people in each network to identify the elements of organizational context that shaped these networks most profoundly.[2] First and foremost, we learned that effective collaboration is a holistic challenge. It is seldom sufficient to simply introduce a collaborative technology, tweak incentives, or advocate cultural programs to promote collaboration. Promoting connectivity requires the alignment of unique aspects of formal organizational design, control systems, technology, and human resource practices. And specific cultural values and leadership behavior can also have a striking effect on patterns of collaboration, often overriding seemingly aligned organizational designs.

Just as important, we learned that there is no one universally correct way to promote connectivity. The right elements of context to work with are unique to each organization. In some settings, it is critical to battle an entrenched cultural value (such as a not-invented-here mentality), whereas in others it is important to modify division-level planning processes and performance metrics. As a result, our model of organizational context is comprehensive so that managers can make informed judgments within their own organizations. While rarely pragmatic to totally reorient your organizations to support a given network, usually five to ten aspects of context provide high-leverage opportunities for improving collaboration. As shown in figure 7-3, we have identified four key categories (elaborated in diagnostic questions in appendix B): your organization's formal structure, work management practices, HR practices, and leadership and culture.

Formal Structure

The first element of organizational context to consider is an organization's formal structure. Following Mintzberg[3] and Galbraith,[4] we think of formal structure as consisting of three major elements: *boundaries* (organizing units such as functions, products, and geography), *decision rights* (the authority to influence behavior and the allocation of resources in an organizing unit), and *integrating mechanisms* (methods for coordinating activities across units). Each of these elements constitutes an opportunity to promote network connectivity.

Boundaries

As we have illustrated, fragmentation in networks often stems from the way work is departmentalized. Overly rigid boundaries within a function, division, or department hamper coordination with and learning

FIGURE 7-3

Social Networks in Context

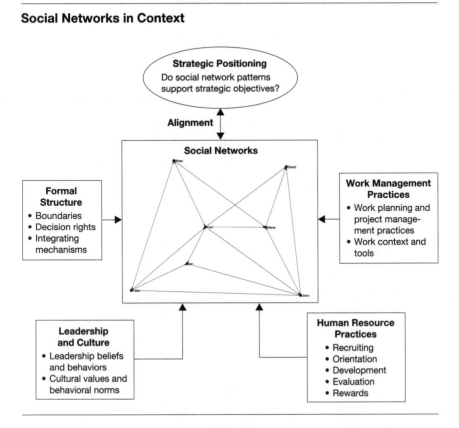

from key stakeholders. Networks that are meant to span organizational boundaries—such as across a core process, a new-product development initiative, or a globally dispersed business unit—often break down at functional or physical boundaries. Where organizations pool expertise to differentiate themselves from competitors, these barriers to collaboration and coordination can critically affect execution of strategy.[5]

When networks fragment at functional or departmental boundaries, the culprit is usually performance metrics that focus a group on its own objectives and provide little incentive for integrating across functional or departmental lines. We often work with groups that have undertaken reengineering initiatives to better integrate functions or divisions yet find minimal cross-group collaboration because they have not reexamined performance metrics. In addition, strategic planning and budgeting processes focus on existing products and services and provide little room for exploring and repackaging expertise across organizational lines.

A first step in resolving these problems is to determine the pattern and level of connectivity—both within and across groups—that will yield success. Once you have identified these patterns, you can ensure that the organization's performance-management systems and planning processes are not impeding network integration. For example, you can build objectives into planning processes to help determine how expertise in a network (or across a series of networks) can be uniquely packaged to meet the needs of the market. Alternatively, you can launch development projects, with measurable objectives, to ensure learning and integration across boundaries.

Decision Rights

As shown in earlier examples, managers can promote network flexibility by reallocating decision rights. Often, simple shifts in who can see what information or who can make what decision can substantially improve a network's flexibility and responsiveness. This same approach can be a powerful way of thinking about organizational design in general. Combining network analysis with traditional tools such as process maps, executives can better design processes and jobs to avoid network overload.

We are currently in the midst of a project with a large retail bank. A senior executive became interested in ensuring optimal interaction patterns among tellers, customer service representatives, loan officers, and branch managers in key retail branches. Mapping all the branches would take too long, so we are working with a small subset that is representative in size and volume of activity. The idea is to apply network techniques to various kinds of information flow and decision making. The bank executives will then be able to replicate the changes in job design and process flow throughout the system.

Mechanisms for Integration

When you need only occasional cross-boundary collaboration, you can establish committees to help ensure appropriate connectivity. If you have frequent coordination issues, it can be critical to designate a liaison or emissary to attend different units' meetings and maintain an awareness of complementary efforts. You can also create intermediary roles—such as a knowledge manager, staffing coordinator, or program manager—to help connect people.

Information itself also can be a vital integrating mechanism. Organizations that invest heavily in enterprise software from vendors such as SAP, PeopleSoft, and Oracle have created multibusiness, multifunctional governance networks to ensure that decentralized units get the information they need while still providing an accurate composite picture at the enterprise level.[6] Rather than vest responsibility in a single officer, such as a CIO, or in a function, such as IT, British Petroleum and Wal-Mart, among others, have worked to establish flexible networks of managers, strategists, and functional experts to guide the installation and continuing refinement of enterprise systems.

Work Management Practices

Work management practices constitute a second element of organizational context that shapes network patterns. One of the most powerful levers managers have for developing effective networks is the group's natural unit of work, whether it be new-product development in pharmaceuticals, a project in professional services, or a financial transaction in investment banking. Working together on a task helps people develop an awareness of colleagues' expertise and a social tie that makes a colleague more likely to help out in a timely fashion. And in contrast to off-site meetings or team-building activities, this development occurs in the pursuit of organizational objectives and so is inexpensive. Thus, the way you frame and staff work can significantly affect network connectivity.

Work Planning and Project Management Practices

Looking for opportunities to carve out assignments so that employees can collaborate often builds relationships and improves solutions. Several consulting organizations have begun to staff two or more people on projects even when it might be more cost-efficient to assign one person for a longer period. Similarly, an information sciences department in a major pharmaceutical organization instituted "team searches" for literature reviews requested by scientists. In this way, the managers broadened the perspectives brought to bear on a given search as well as strengthened the department's network. This company and others report that focusing on collaborative opportunities instead of on individual accountability improves problem solving, employee morale, and network connectivity.

Project management can also have a significant effect. First, practices can encourage employees to reach out to experts in the organization when projects are initiated. Organizations we assessed that encouraged and evaluated this behavior promoted network connectivity, teamwork, and better solutions. Second, project managers and project management methodologies can incorporate reflection and learning activities, such as after-action reviews, during a project. These exercises improve the work of the team and network connectivity as people learn more about their colleagues' expertise.

It's also important for managers to consider formal project management methodologies or process steps at points where work in progess moves from one function to another. Often, either norms or formal processes and procedures undermine effective collaboration between functions. In several organizations we worked with, work in progress was handed off without mechanisms to establish shared understanding and context. As a result, the function taking over often had trouble executing the work.

Work Context and Tools

Physical context can dramatically affect collaboration.[7] One of the most well established findings in the social sciences is that distance impedes communication: The farther two people are from each other, the less likely they are to collaborate.[8] Throughout our research, we have found that physical space—distance between potential collaborators and other barriers, such as hall layout or office design—has a dramatic effect on who interacts with whom. For example, at a technology organization, our network analysis showed that tall cubicle walls were blocking communication between two teams. When the walls were lowered, the teams discovered greater commonality in their work and pushed for additional space for shared brainstorming.

Often, expense prohibits face-to-face gatherings in distributed networks. Technologies can be effective at promoting collaboration if the organization's culture encourages their use and if members can find the right medium for a given task. For example, IBM has various consulting practices whose members rarely, if ever, meet face-to-face. These groups have learned to rely on various collaborative technologies. Consultants often supplement large-scale operational conference calls with the use of Lotus Instant Messaging and Web Conferencing (a synchronous collaborative tool formerly called Sametime). This tool supports one-on-one or small-group interactions for problem solving and clarification. In other instances, employees combine conference calls with NetMeeting, which allows distant colleagues to collectively see and work on a presentation. In this way, workers can brainstorm visually as well as verbally. The trick is to develop skill with the technology and to establish norms for its use. Unfortunately, we often found technologies going unused because employees preferred to wait for face-to-face interactions or didn't understand how technology could be an acceptable substitute.

We have waited until this chapter to talk about technology because we want to emphasize that promoting effective collaboration in organizations is first and foremost a human issue. Rather than make the mistake of early reengineering efforts—claiming that technology is an enabler but placing it at the forefront of process design—executives are better off understanding how work gets done and how relationships develop in their organization and then finding ways to enhance these processes with technical applications. Under those circumstances, technology can help networks become productive, and we have seen the following applications have a substantial effect on network connectivity.

Instant Messaging

Teenagers are well aware of the benefits of instant messaging (IM), and the corporate world is quickly catching on. IM's primary benefit is that it supports the serendipity of hallway conversations in large, distributed groups. Although not as rich as face-to-face communication, IM enables people to have fluid one-on-one as well as group discussions. People can ask questions when they have them rather than forgetting or deciding that pursuing a line of thought is too much work. And IM is cheap and easy to use. We have been amazed at the impact of this inexpensive technology that in its own way enables virtual "coffee machine" or "water cooler" conversations. We often hear people describe how IM let them collaborate with a colleague in the early, critical stages of forming an innovative idea or solving a tough problem.

Beyond one-to-one connection, we have also seen the effect of IM on large networks. For example, we conducted a network analysis of a large software development group in a major technology company that was a high user of IM. It turned out that this group was well connected overall, but in particular it was the very best connected group across distance that we have seen. This connectivity (and various benefits coming from it) was especially surprising because almost half the group members worked in satellite offices (including home-based offices) around the country. All the people we interviewed attributed the success of this arrangement to widespread use of IM.

Skill-Profiling Systems

Instant messaging works well when you know whom you want to collaborate with. But what happens when we are confronted with projects or problems requiring new and different expertise? Skill-profiling or expertise locator systems are the equivalent of online resumes. They allow people to find others with relevant skills, even if they don't know them. Of course, these systems are helpful only if employees update their profiles. As a result, establishing and maintaining these systems require effort on the part of an organization (though applications are emerging that generate profiles automatically based on scanning and categorization of e-mail traffic).

Skill-profiling systems can greatly improve connectivity in large, distributed networks. However, we found that this potential was realized only in organizations where the systems were implemented with an eye to how people gain credibility in a setting. Failing to take this into account was a significant shortcoming in most of the organizations we worked with. One consulting organization was unique in providing information about people in ways that encouraged seekers to trust in their expertise. This organization paid little heed to academic degrees but was highly interested in where people had applied their expertise in recent engagements. Employee profiles therefore included each person's three to five most recent projects and the names of people they had worked with so that seekers might also find someone they knew who knew the person listed.

The most effective systems we have seen include whatever confers credibility in a given work setting. In some companies, for example, academic degrees mark people's expertise; in others it's publications or patents or specific project experience. Each profession and organization has its own set of credentials that demonstrate expertise. Instead of simply following the predefined structures, you will gain more from the application by customizing it so that whatever confers expertise in your setting is central to the system.

But simply knowing that someone has expertise does not guarantee that he or she will return your call. As summarized in chapter 6, including personal information in a profile (e.g., a common hobby or alma mater) often helps people find points of connection that prompt an expert to return a call. These points of commonality also often help get a conversation with an expert going.

Group Support Systems

Synchronous (same-time) Web-conferencing products like Microsoft's NetMeeting have numerous functionalities, such as chat and file transfer, remote desktop and program sharing, white boards, and video and audio conferencing. These technologies allow for (virtual) real-time interaction while people work on a document together. They are a significant improvement over traditional conference calls, in which many of the participants remain faceless and collaboration is typically low.

Asynchronous technologies, such as team rooms, also promote collaboration by letting people store documents in one accessible place—not only on individuals' hard drives—and alerting others to documents that require their attention. Team rooms keep everyone up-to-date on a project. They also allow people to contribute their knowledge and skills on parts of a project that others may not have known they had skills in. This ensures that people are not left isolated on the periphery of a team and that the skills of the group are used to their maximum.

E-mail Applications

We are all familiar with e-mail, but new applications that can be attached to e-mail, such as KnowledgeMail, have transformed this familiar technology. KnowledgeMail, made by Tacit, analyzes e-mail correspondence in an organization to find out who is working on what and who the experts are on a particular subject. The software creates an expertise profile not only for each person but also each department and system, and it updates its databases continuously.

Human Resource Practices

The entire human resources chain can affect collaboration by influencing the kinds of people hired, the way they are developed, and the behaviors that are measured and rewarded. The first question we ask managers to consider is this: "Do you recruit on the basis of individual accomplishment, personal chemistry, or demonstration of collaborative behaviors?" A frequent distinguishing feature of more cohesive networks is that the managers recruit for collaborative behaviors. For example, they might employ a critical-incident technique to seek evidence of collaborative behaviors. Alternatively, some organizations require recruits to demonstrate collaborative behavior in the hiring process through a group problem-solving exercise. In the words of one manager, "The problem solving in these things is horrific, but you get a very, very accurate view of who is going to work well in a collaborative environment." The key is to make sure that hiring decisions are to some degree influenced by what is learned during the recruiting process; it does no good to interview for these behaviors but then base the final hiring decision on individual accomplishment or personal chemistry.

A second question we often pose to managers is, "Do your orientation practices actively help new people integrate into the organization?" Integrating new hires quickly and smoothly seems to require two things: helping new people meet established network members and helping existing members become aware of the new person's expertise. Managers of cohesive networks tend to employ both kinds of practices systematically instead of leaving them to chance. For example, some companies rotate new people through different departments in their first few weeks. Others have structured introductions whereby key managers take new people to lunch in small groups during the first two weeks. Rather than being only a nice gesture, these lunches are a formal part of orientation and are set up in advance of the new hire's arrival. They are an opportunity for managers and new employees to establish a personal connection and for managers to learn more about the organization's newly acquired expertise. This is crucial because new people are generally drawn into networks by more established people who are aware of their expertise.

Executives should also consider the extent to which certain approaches to training and professional development can help employees build personal networks. Many organizations conduct training in a group setting (instead of sending individuals to external programs), and this practice supports not only knowledge transfer but also the development of relationships between people engaged in similar work throughout the organization. Furthermore, professional development programs can help employees nurture and sustain effective personal networks.[9] Several organizations we work with use the career development process to help employees assess the current composition of their networks and develop targeted plans to improve connectivity. Such an approach provides critical grassroots support for integrating networks at given junctures.

Performance evaluation is also an important HR process that can promote collaboration at critical points in networks. Some organizations use project-level performance appraisals that assess an employee's collaborative behavior on a given project. Others employ annual evaluations requiring people to demonstrate that they have supported cross-division efforts. Still others use 360-degree evaluation processes that ask people from other units whether they have been supported by a certain person. Whichever approach you choose, such programs are worthwhile only if they are taken seriously and if those assessing an individual's collaborative behaviors have credibility with the person being assessed. Ideally, those conducting assessments have direct experience with the person (unlike a manager, who may have interacted with the person for only part of a project).

The final and perhaps most important question we pose to managers is, "Do you reward collaborative behaviors or focus heavily on individual accomplishment?" Formal rewards signal whether collaboration or individual achievement is important. Considering who has gotten promoted recently or who receives the biggest bonuses can be a telling indicator of the kind of behaviors management values. Alternatively, you might assess the components of a performance evaluation that really matter in pay raises. It is counterproductive and little more than rhetoric to advocate the need for collaboration and sharing and then show employees what really matters with reward systems that run counter to sharing or helping colleagues.

Formal reward systems are only one way—and perhaps not even the most effective way—to acknowledge people who go out of their way to help colleagues. Public spot rewards such as bonuses, dinners, or gift certificates can be powerful means of promoting collaboration. Even more substantial are the opportunities that managers can create to bestow respect on individuals and teams. For example, General

Motors has recently reinstituted "garage shows" in its technical centers. These events are reminiscent of the informal open houses that auto mechanics and hot-rodders organize to show off their inventions.

Unfortunately, too often we found that spot rewards were given out only in recognition of heroic effort, such as an employee putting in long hours to complete a project. Rarely did we hear about someone being recognized for having gone out of his or her way to help others.

Leadership and Culture

Leadership and culture can either support or nullify the best network designs. We found some leaders who were capable of promoting rich, highly flexible networks underneath them. Instead of consolidating a position of authority, these leaders shared information and decision-making responsibility, connected the people around them, and drew peripheral people in. But we also found leaders who created sparse networks isolated from the broader organization and overly dependent on the leader. For example, at a travel services company we encountered the paradox of a dynamic and visionary leader who micromanaged to the point that he was draining the life and spontaneity from the very networks that had enabled the firm to leap ahead of its online competitors.

The first major difference between more effective and less effective leaders was how they thought about their own work and that of their employees. Less effective network builders tended to focus on individual accountability and broke tasks into small, often individual, chunks. More effective leaders envisioned tasks as challenges sufficiently large and complex that they demanded collaboration. In general, this belief in the importance of collaboration carried over into problem-solving sessions in which everyone's opinions were sought, regardless of hierarchy or experience. It was also evident in continuing efforts to engage people on the periphery of a network in direct projects or other opportunities to help get them more integrated.

These leaders also tended to celebrate effective collaboration. In our interviews, we asked people whether success stories that spread through their organization were more likely to be about a person who handles a crisis well or overcomes significant odds (a hero) or a person who is collaborative and finds ways to involve and help others. Not surprisingly, the hero usually got all the attention. Leaders can change this phenomenon by virtue of what they recognize. We found that in better-connected networks, leaders acknowledged collaborative work in public forums, congratulated those who went out of their way for others, or promoted people who were collaborators. In both word and action, these leaders sent unambiguous signals about the importance of collaboration. The key for managers is to identify the collaborative behaviors that can build network connectivity in their organizations and then systematically recognize and reward them.

The second difference we found was that leaders of better-connected networks tended to be more aware of interpersonal tensions within the network. This did not mean that they themselves were highly skilled at correcting interpersonal tensions or improving political dynamics; often they brought in facilitators. However, they had the awareness and courage to deal early on with tough interpersonal issues (either between themselves and others, or among members in their group) rather than ignore the issues and let them fester. In contrast, less effective leaders often knew of interpersonal tensions but chose not to proactively address such situations in hopes that they would disappear. Unfortunately, such problems don't usually go away, and we often saw tensions between managers radiate down in a network and create fissures between entire groups.

The final differentiating feature we found between leaders was that network-building leaders were generally strong communicators and advocates of communication and face-to-face interaction. Often in nationally or globally distributed groups, the only relationships that bridge geographic, functional, or hierarchical boundaries are a product of people having interacted in person. When cost precludes travel, various technologies can be applied, but generally with less success in helping to establish relationships that people later rely on.

But not all face-to-face interaction is created equal. The forums that work best for network building are not the standard operational status meeting or quarterly review, where people listen to presentations and then mingle at a cocktail hour with those they already know. At the more successful forums—exemplified by quarterly management conferences at companies such as Nucor Corporation[10]—people read material beforehand and use their precious time together for collaborative problem solving. For example, employees form teams from various functions or physical locations, and these groups not only solve problems but also help to form relationships across boundaries. These relationships often last beyond that meeting, thereby creating a more robust network.

Finally, it is important to consider culture—both occupational and organizational—because it can override collaborative behaviors encouraged by the formal design. In one sense culture is generated and transmitted through social networks. Yet it also sits outside of and constrains networks via established norms of practices. An important role of leadership is to communicate, model, and reward behaviors that counter unproductive tendencies. If left unattended, incongruence between cultural values and desired patterns of collaboration is sure to derail management efforts.

How does culture undermine management efforts to support collaboration? First, culture operates via occupational identification. Network assessments often reflect subgroups formed by people who care about the same dimensions of their work. Such people are naturally drawn to similar issues and tend to enjoy easier communication and collaboration. For example, marketing people care and talk about market potential or sales, whereas engineers often care about and debate the quality of their product. Such subgroups can become insular to the point that cross-functional collaboration is impeded as these groups lose an ability to visualize how their work fits together. One way of overcoming such local tendencies is to nurture commitment to a superordinate goal such as protecting the country (at the Navy) or curing health problems (at the World Bank). Alternatively, leaders can set performance objectives that can be achieved only by working differently, a stratagem employed effectively by companies such as GE and Honda.

Specific cultural values also can preclude effective collaboration. Often, these norms are the unintended consequence of values that once made sense but have never been revisited. For example, the not-invented-here syndrome may be rooted in a history of successful invention and self-reliance that has evolved unchecked. Alternatively, cultures that have become excessively contentious or political are rarely populated by mean, self-interested ogres; instead, they lack effective norms of conflict resolution that allow people to "lose" without humiliation. Neither of these cultural obstacles to collaboration is intentional, but they form the unwritten rules that guide day-to-day behavior.[11]

Nationality can also play a substantial role in network patterns. Most of the examples in this book come from North American companies, with a few examples from Europe, Australia, Canada, and South America. Even with this limited international view, we have seen some tendencies that seem to be a result of national norms. For example, the three Canadian companies we worked with had dense network patterns. Interviews revealed a much more collaborative and consultative mind-set than seemed to exist in U.S. companies in the same industries. We have also noted insular and sparse networks in some of the European countries. Interviews in these settings suggest values that drive more closed and politically oriented networks.

Setting the Stage

When managers combine network analysis with attention to organizational context—formal structure, work management practices, human resource policies, leadership, and culture—they can ensure that employees' efforts are aligned with strategic imperatives and that networks will not fall back into unproductive patterns over time. We are not suggesting a reorganization encompassing all dimensions of organizational context. Rather, managers should view our framing as a set of practices from which they can select ones that are under their control and are most appropriate for their organization. In crafting a supportive context, it is critical to bear in mind that knowledge-intensive work is largely emergent. Instead of attempting to design for an unknown future with great precision, managers are advised to create a context that supports effective innovation and collaboration.

To this point we have provided a way for managers to leverage informal networks in their organizations for better collaboration and information sharing across boundaries. Chapters 1 to 4 demonstrate how managers can find and fix disconnects, enhance information flow, and create energy that fuels the work of the organization. Chapters 5 to 7 describe a framework for making corrections when social network analysis identifies opportunities for improvement, first through actions geared toward the individuals in the network, then through the relationships between individuals across the network, and finally through the organizational context. In chapter 8 we offer a view of future network trends in organizations as well as some cautions concerning networks and network analysis. Although we are optimistic about the future of a network perspective in organizations, those who invest time and effort in the pursuit of these ideas should do so with an eye to potential drawbacks or resistance they might encounter.

8

Uncharted Territory

The Future and Challenges of Networks
in Organizations

W HETHER PEOPLE use the term or not, networks are an essential feature of organizations, responsible in large part for organizational effectiveness and innovation.[1] As a result, we see a bright
future for networks both within and between organizations. In terms
of interorganizational relationships, we believe that there will be an
increased use of social network analysis to assess the effectiveness of
strategic partnerships. Joint ventures, alliances, and R&D consortia
typically are undertaken to promote innovation and to quickly integrate capabilities on a specific initiative. However, little attention has
been paid to the social networks created in these entities and to the
ways they can help fulfill such goals. Network analysis, applied to both
information flow and decision making in strategic partnerships, can
dramatically improve the effectiveness of these corporate junctures, as
outlined in chapter 2.

Beyond a single alliance or partnership, we expect to see network
analysis increasingly applied to an organization's entire set of partnerships. Strategic advantage can come not only from negotiating one or
two alliances but also from taking a network perspective and locking in
a constellation of relationships in which decisions relating to one
alliance can open up or constrain opportunities with other potential
partners.[2] This is a shift in perspective and strategic decision making
that one of our colleagues characterizes as moving from running a bat-
tleship to orchestrating an armada. And the perspective can be broadened to include an organization's relationships with customers, suppli-
ers, and employees. This holistic view of an organization's "relational

131

capital" can be seen as a key strategic resource and can be related to financial outcomes through network analysis.[3]

We also expect to see leaders place greater emphasis (in either a planned or a haphazard way) on promoting social networks and seamless collaboration within organizations. In some organizations this might occur on a broad scale, such as GE's efforts to become "boundaryless." In others it might simply mean the use of ad hoc committees or collaborative technologies. We can only expect competitive forces to demand more effective collaboration from organizations. What we suggest throughout this book is that a targeted effort to support appropriate connectivity will yield better results than one-time or broadbrush approaches.

As networks become a more recognized part of organizational life, ideas about them will certainly evolve and efforts to improve them should become more targeted and sophisticated. In the future we expect to see networks designed with an eye to specific value propositions. For example, a network designed to provide highly customized services or expertise might have a dense pattern of connectivity, with incentives and technologies that allow the group to sense customers' needs and rapidly respond with relevant expertise regardless of physical locale or functional niche. In contrast, a network designed to provide routine low-cost solutions will be more efficient if it has fewer relationships, more compartmentalization, and a technical infrastructure to support repetitive work. These are only two of numerous possible network configurations with markedly different value propositions, economics, and infrastructure.

At an individual level, we also foresee executives paying greater attention to personal connectivity (both their own and their employees'). Adoption of tools such as Act! and Outlook, which help people manage personal contacts, is rapidly increasing. And human resource departments in some leading organizations have begun to make individual network assessment and development a part of their career development processes.

In particular, we believe that managing personal network connectivity will become an increasingly important part of developing high performers. The great bulk of information on which executives take action comes from their personal networks. Being an effective decision maker, particularly as you move higher in an organization, means being able to receive diverse information and weigh perspectives and opinions. Time and again, we have heard executives describe making decisions and then encountering substantial resistance because they had not considered the needs of certain constituents or all aspects of an initiative. Exposure to diverse views is critical for executives, but it is difficult to achieve because much of their schedule is dictated to them. Network analysis is one means of ensuring that personal networks do not become too heavily biased or insular.

Changes Ahead

Network Dynamics

As work has become more project-specific, flexible, and short-term, the work force as a whole has become more mobile.[4] In addition, managerial initiatives such as delayering, reengineering, and team-based designs (to name only a few) have diminished the role of formally prescribed relationships in organizations. The result is that employee networks are not as static as communication or information flow diagrams generated as part of a social network analysis might suggest. But so far, managers have paid little attention to the more dynamic characteristics of networks and the ways that dynamic qualities of networks affect organizational flexibility and change.[5]

In several cases, we have mapped networks at two points in time and have seen dramatic shifts in patterns even after a brief interval. For example, an assessment of information scientists on two occasions revealed strikingly different patterns of collaboration as a result of a reorganization that merged groups and altered roles and responsibilities. However, despite the shift in patterns of information flow, we found that some relationships had not dissolved, causing the network to become overloaded. People who became central after the reorganization were being tapped for information related to both their new *and* their previous roles.

We have seen similar results in organizations that try to integrate after a merger or that have adopted team-based designs. Organizational charts can be redrawn quickly, but, in reality, it takes time for some relationships to fade away and other trusted contacts to develop. To facilitate change, network analysts will need to better address both enduring and dynamic aspects of relationships.

Computer simulations of networks can also reveal potential network dynamics and inform the strategic and logistical decisions made by managers. These simulations can be highly informative if managers can collect relevant data and have the skills to devise and run the software. On a simpler level, network scenarios based on the departure of certain people or classes of people can show executives where their organization might be vulnerable. This is a serious issue when the job market is hot, as it was in the late 1990s. It is also a current issue in government, where massive retirements loom. Network analysis can help managers prepare for departures by building appropriate redundancies into the network.

A Deeper View of Relationships

This book focuses principally on information flow and collaboration, a common theme in network studies. Although some researchers have looked at the emotional aspects of networks, such as friendship, liking, or trust,[6] most have paid attention to the structural properties of networks. We think that one trend in network analysis will be toward mapping different, theoretically important dimensions of relationships.

We are working on one aspect of this with Bill Kahn of Boston University by assessing the various functions of workplace relationships. To date, we have conducted sixty interviews in three organizations, asking people about the relationships they turn to for various needs at work. Beginning with a blank piece of paper, our interviewees describe whom they rely on, both within and outside their organization, for the following:

- Task purposes—people who provide information, resources, or direction that helps us get work done

- Career development (learning)—people who give feedback that is helpful for our career development

- Career support (political support)—people in influential positions who are advocates and provide political support

- Sense making—people who help make sense of rumors, events, or gossip

- Personal support—people who help us cope with and recover from troubling situations at work or personal dilemmas

- Purpose—people who make us feel that what we do at work matters, that our work has meaning

Our interviewees consistently indicate that they need people in their lives who can serve each of these purposes. And although the relationship functions become increasingly abstract as we move down the list, the deeper functions are often considered the most important. Most interesting, though, is the variety of ways that people manage the sets of relationships serving these functions. For example, some have extensive task networks but rely on only one or two people for the other functions. They are often surprised to learn how seriously their network would be disrupted by the loss of only one key contact. Others have highly diversified networks and are precise about whom they turn to for what. Theirs are more robust networks, but these interviewees are quick to acknowledge the time and effort it takes to maintain a high number of unique relationships.

The point of this research is in part to help people diagnose the effectiveness of their networks by providing a deeper view of relationships. However, what someone's network should look like depends on a number of factors we are just beginning to explore. For example, the way people leverage relationships seems to depend on where they are in their careers. Early on, most of them have robust career development networks and rely on the customer and the boss for a sense of purpose. Later, career development networks are less important than sense-making ones, and purpose tends to come from respected colleagues or people outside the organization, such as family members. In our next series of projects, we hope to gain greater insight into how personality, job design, career stage, and gender might suggest certain patterns of relationships that will result in more effective and satisfied people.

We have also mapped these dimensions in groups, with some interesting results. For example, in considering a virtual network of experts in a technology organization, we learned that telecommuters readily got information and help through virtual social networks. However, they struggled mightily to obtain deeper benefits such as personal support and purpose. It seems that face-to-face interaction, and possibly the trust that accrues from such interactions, is necessary if off-site workers are to gain personal benefits from relationships.

In a different setting, we found that these relationship dimensions uniquely predict job satisfaction and employee commitment. Position in the sense-making and career development networks led to greater job satisfaction—but not in the way you might think. People reported that it was having people come to them for these things that predicted satisfaction, not having others to turn to. This finding holds interesting implications for mentoring programs. At least in terms of satisfaction, it suggests that such programs do more for the mentor than for the mentee.

This work is leading us to a more rounded view of how employees rely on the relationships around them. Other important work we are aware of on this front has begun to focus on negative aspects of relationships in organizations.[7] Rather than assume that all relationships are helpful, this work posits the idea that negative relationships, though potentially few in number, have a stronger impact than helpful ones. And network views can be taken beyond people-to-people interactions. Kathleen Carley of Carnegie Mellon has long advocated considering various databases or other information sources as network nodes.

Enabling Technology

Perhaps the single biggest contributor to the recent rise of social network analysis is the advance in computing capabilities. At a tactical level, some of the most important developments right now are in data collection and representation. We can now construct networks from e-mail correspondence and even mine e-mail communications to better understand the content of the interactions. Although e-mail mining raises ethical dilemmas and indeed has legal boundaries, it can give us a greater understanding of networks across entire organizations.

Using agent-based technology, you can build a profile of a person on the basis of the content of e-mails and documents flowing across e-mail servers. In a fairly unobtrusive way, organizations can use these systems to generate a profile of expertise and thus help people to find experts. Although networks created through e-mail interactions might reflect only one medium and not face-to-face interaction (which many people consider to be the most vital medium), the importance of this technology cannot be discounted. If these systems become widely used, they could have a substantial impact on traditional social networks. For example, if people are ultimately connecting more through technology than they are in person, they may be connecting more on tasks and less on personal similarities or organizational affiliation. This means that, on the one hand, employee networks might become more fluid and responsive. On the other hand, people might be tempted to game the system, hoarding information and claiming expertise in ways that elevate their profile but do not help the organization.

Another issue is the effective representation of complex network information. To have an impact, network information must be simplified but meaningful on both an individual and a group level. Various software tools help here, both in data collection and representation of information. Data-mining tools such as Raison, which was developed at IBM's Watson Laboratories, crawls databases that contain individual-level information and then aggregates it for analysis at the organizational level. Network drawing packages such as Pajek use sophisticated algorithms to condense networks of hundreds of thousands of nodes into smaller, more manageable networks that can be analyzed using more specific methods.

Potential Drawbacks of a Network Perspective

There are, of course, limits to the usefulness of a network perspective. The organizations with which we have worked are far from this point. But as the idea of networks becomes increasingly popular, managers should consider potential drawbacks. Networks are only one piece of a complex puzzle, but as network thinking gains momentum the approach could become a fad—the Next Big Thing. If this happens, social network analysis may not be applied in a measured way. Focusing exclusively on social networks is dangerous if people believe that optimal networks alone will lead to the Holy Grail of high performance. Clearly, other issues are important. For example, hiring, developing, and retaining skilled people are critical. So are databases and other information stores. Databases, although not the first stop for most people, still provide a powerful form of memory, routines, and reusable work products.

It can also be dangerous for managers to focus too closely on collaborative tools. For example, we have seen managers force people to use instant messaging technologies, with the unintended result that employees spent so much time corresponding that their work suffered. In fact, tools that allow for easy connectivity pose some danger to relationships. Although it's easy to send an instant message or e-mail to another person when you have the time, it might not be as timely or easy for the recipient to respond appropriately. Yet responding curtly two days late—or, worse, deleting e-mails late at night in frustration— can quickly harm or sever a relationship. An e-mail sent and not responded to indexes the relationship to the sender, even though the recipient might not even remember deleting the message. And he or she may never have a chance to repair the misunderstanding.

In addition, social networks are only one aspect of social capital worthy of consideration. Culture, in terms of shared values and meaning, is intertwined with networks in various ways and represents another important lever for managers. We see this often in terms of trust or safety in organizations. In some places it is perfectly acceptable for employees to ask for help. In others, such requests are seen as a sign of weakness or incompetence. This has less to do with network patterns than with the culture of a given organization or occupation.

Limitations of Social Network Analysis

Social network analysis as a managerial tool also has its limits and potential drawbacks. To be sure, network analysis captures a detailed view of work and collaboration that other diagnostics cannot provide. However, network analysis alone can teach us only so much. In addition, networks are highly revealing, and network analysts have a responsibility to ensure ethical use of the information. This is particularly true when people or departments are cast in a less than positive light. In these situations, analysts must be skilled not only in collecting and analyzing network information but also in presenting results constructively and facilitating a dialog to improve network patterns.

Limitations of Network Information

Getting good network information is always a challenge. Some ways of collecting network data place little burden on people in the network. For example, using e-mail logs to assess connectivity is quick and easy. However, the conduits that are easiest to analyze may not be the ones that carry critical information. Put a network of e-mail traffic in front of an executive and he or she will tell you that the diagram does not capture important information flows. Rather, executives are much more likely to be engaged with a network of face-to-face interactions where the bulk of their work happens. To get to more meaningful levels of interaction, data can be collected through observation or electronic nametags that communicate with each other. These methods can provide greater precision, but they carry a cost.

We find that excessive detail is overkill for addressing managerial concerns about social networks. In most cases, we obtain highly useful network information through surveys. But even these take time, depending on the size of the group, and are subject to problems of survey-based research. People can forget important relationships when they're hurrying to complete a survey. They can misreport interactions, inflating their responses to make themselves look more central. And each diagram reflects only one aspect of a relationship.

Appendix A outlines ways to validate survey-based information, such as asking both parties about an interaction. Analysts can also combine networks to learn more about the inner workings of a group. However, to be truly helpful, action items for improving network connectivity must be developed in close collaboration with knowledgeable network members. Typically, either in meetings with a few members or in full-group facilitated sessions, we illustrate points in the network that we think are effective or problematic and then ask members which issues matter to them. It is important for network analysts not to get caught up in the seeming precision of the diagrams and analytics until they have checked their conclusions with members of the network.

Another limit of network analysis is the expertise of the analyst. It takes time to develop experience in all aspects of the process—from selecting a group to designing and administering a survey to analyzing and providing feedback—and there are many mistakes that can be made. We have made most if not all of them somewhere in this journey. In appendix A, we have tried to be precise while not overbearing in delineating important steps and considerations in network analysis. But each group poses new challenges, and judgment plays a role each time we conduct an analysis. Interpreting network information is also as much art as science; a colleague equates this to the difference between being able to take an X ray and being able to interpret it. Developing the ability to spot problem points takes time, although systematically walking through each analysis is a good way to gain this experience.

Misinterpretation of Network Diagrams

There is something mythical and compelling about network diagrams. Even when we don't know the people or issues a group is wrestling with, the diagrams speak to us on an intuitive level. We just know that they reflect how work is really getting done. However, the diagrams can appear complex to someone looking at them for the first time, and occasionally managers will read into them what they want to see and overlook what the information is actually suggesting.

We will never forget a debriefing with a high-level executive and his management team. We had created a network diagram of connections that *did not* exist but should exist for the group to be successful. Not hearing us indicate that these were nonexistent relationships, the manager immediately began recounting events and happenings that had created that specific network. During a five-minute monologue, he recalled interactions—from a ropes course to prior work lives to current projects—that he was sure had generated the network pattern in front of him. The message here is that these diagrams are compelling sense-making devices, and we must be careful not to let our beliefs and wishes take over.

To help avoid misinterpretations, it is important that a network analyst be systematic about sharing the results. And the analyst should develop a low-key way of correcting the occasional inaccurate reading of a diagram. This can be tricky if the errant interpreter is a senior executive, but it is critical to correct these inaccuracies early. The extent to which these diagrams stay in managers' minds and shift how they think and talk about employees is remarkable. Even when an organization does not take immediate action on these ideas, we are always amazed at the shift in language and ways of thinking about groups of employees and personal connectivity after managers have been exposed to network ideas.

Defensiveness

Network diagrams, more so than cultural diagnostics or employee opinion surveys, can be highly revealing. Occasionally, network information can evoke defensiveness in and denials from managers or departments that are cast in a less than favorable light. In the worst scenarios, feedback sessions devolve into arguments over network measurement or other concerns that are less important than the problems that are driving poor collaboration.

Analysts can prepare for this to some degree at the beginning of a network analysis. Conducting interviews before the assessment can reveal the political climate. If it is highly charged, we recommend not disclosing names in the diagrams (see appendix A for an in-depth discussion of issues concerning disclosure). You can learn a lot by using different shapes to highlight nodes in network diagrams. These nodes can illuminate, for example, the effect of hierarchy or function. Density tables such as those described in chapter 2 can also be informative without revealing names. Although the energy level in a room is usually higher if the diagrams contain people's names, it is always better not to present unnecessarily inflammatory information.

Even when such precautions are taken, most people who engage in this work have stories to tell of managers who were upset by the way they were represented in a network diagram. Our approach here is to focus on systemic, organizational forces that might be driving a person into a given position rather than on what the individual is doing to cause the problem. Productive discussions will grind to a halt if you ask a manager how his or her behavior is adversely affecting connectivity and collaboration.

Focusing on the system rather than the individual can make tough conversations possible and productive for an entire group. For example, overly central people sometimes become bottlenecks because of their own actions but also because others bring myriad questions and decisions to them. Alternatively, sometimes people are on the periphery because they are not heard; their ideas might be correct, but they have not yet proven themselves and so are not listened to. Discussing these issues in the aggregate, not simply casting blame on the individual, can move a group toward collective agreement on the causes of a problem and ways to fix it. Getting someone to agree that he or she has become a bottleneck and must let go of some decision-making power is only part of the battle. You also must get others to agree to stop bringing too many questions and decisions to these people, thus pushing them back into a bottleneck position.

Ethical Considerations

Network analysis, in the worst cases, can be used to hurt people. Those who begin conducting assessments will invariably get requests at some point to use network analysis as a way to identify the people a manager wants to keep, particularly in acquisitions or large-scale change efforts. The real agenda in such situations is to use network analysis to find out whom to fire, usually those on the periphery. As we discussed in chapter 5, there are many reasons that peripheral people may be highly productive. Indiscriminately trying to get rid of peripheral people is not only wrong from an ethical standpoint but also silly from a managerial one.

Even overly central people can be vulnerable. In one instance we were surprised by the vehemence with which an executive focused on a highly central person in a network of an alliance. At first glance, the network diagram indicated that this person was overly connected with many of the people from the alliance partner but less connected with her own organization. This politically motivated executive began to use this information to move the central person to the side. When the sponsor of the network analysis heard what was going on, he showed the executive the original network diagram and a second one with this person removed. The second diagram indicated that without this person, the alliance would fragment. Thankfully, this central person was given some much needed support. However, the danger always exists that network information can be used for destructive purposes by those with a political agenda.

This risk is by no means unique to network analysis, but we sound a cautionary note to those who engage in this work. To the extent possible, it is incumbent on us all to make sure that network information is used ethically and productively for all parties. We have flatly rejected requests to conduct a network analysis when we knew that the organization was preparing for layoffs. We hope it is apparent by now that network analysis should not be used as a basis for such decisions. An analysis can be one piece of data that managers factor in to personnel decisions. But network information, as we have shown, is highly nuanced, and a person's network position must not be the sole determinant of his or her livelihood.

The Road Ahead

Despite limitations and precautions, it should be obvious by now that we think social network analysis has a bright future in organizations. Applied well and in a measured fashion, it holds tremendous potential to improve organizational and individual performance. We hope that others share this enthusiasm and enjoy exploring network ideas as much as we have.

Appendix A

Conducting and Interpreting a Social Network Analysis

T HERE ARE TWO APPROACHES to conducting a social network analysis: personal (egocentric) and group (bounded) network assessments. The *personal* network approach requests a person to identify other people who are important for a given function or task (such as learning or information) and then answer a set of questions regarding each of these people. Relationships in a personal network can come from any and all walks of life, including employees in the same business unit, colleagues elsewhere in the organization, people in entirely different organizations, or friends and family members.

An important advantage of the personal network approach is that it uncovers all relationships that are important to a person (and not only connections to others in one's organization). Data collection, consisting of short surveys, is fast and inexpensive. However, because people often rely on various sets of relationships, you usually cannot create network diagrams of entire divisions or functions by using a personal network approach. Two people in the same organization are likely to identify contacts outside the organization, but because they are not likely to list exactly the same people, it is difficult to create network maps like those in this book.[1]

With the *group* (or *bounded*) network approach, you first define a network of interest, such as a critical function in an organization or a group of people who are integral to a core process. Then you survey each person in the group about his or her relationship with every other member of that group. In contrast to the personal network approach, here you provide the list of names from the group you decide to survey. Although this information can be obtained in a variety of ways, from tracking e-mails to observing people over time, often the most efficient means is to administer a short survey. This can be done through pencil and paper, e-mail attachments, or Web-based tools. It usually takes ten to thirty minutes to complete the survey, depending on the size of the network and the number of questions asked.

Using the complete set of relationships within a group, an analyst can create network maps and apply a variety of quantitative assessments. However, the survey approach can be time-consuming for large groups and does not account for all the connections each person has. For example, a network member could have few connections within the group and thus appear peripheral in the network but have a large and valuable personal network outside the group. Research scientists, salespeople, and subject-matter experts often fall into this category.

Given the importance of understanding external connections, we combine both group and personal network approaches when we conduct a network assessment. This allows managers to assess external links, which can be critical sources of new information and ideas (such as R&D units closely connected to academic institutions) or can reveal points where network insularity is a potential problem (for example, where leaders or entire groups focus only on each other and do not bring in information from the outside). It also provides diagnostic information that individuals within the network can use to develop an effective personal network.

Conducting a Social Network Analysis

Step 1: Identify a Strategically Important Group

The first step in conducting a network analysis is to identify a network in which effective collaboration is important for an organization. Sometimes, formally designated functions or departments are good choices. For example, R&D groups in pharmaceutical organizations or commercial lending functions in banks can, on their own, provide substantial insight for managers. However, you can usually gain greater benefits if you consider networks that don't reside on the formal organizational chart and so receive little executive attention or resources. For example, assessing the intersection of R&D *and* marketing functions in pharmaceutical organizations can have a much more powerful impact on drug development and launch than analyzing R&D on its own. Similarly, considering the network across the entire commercial lending process can help executives identify cross-selling opportunities or reduce loan cycle times much more effectively than assessing only the commercial lending function.

We urge people to consider groups in which effective collaboration yields strategic and operational benefits to an organization. We also look for groups that cross functional, hierarchical, and physical boundaries because these are very common fragmentation points in networks. Typical applications in the organizations we have worked with include the following.

- *Integrating Networks That Cross Core Processes.* Networks across core processes are often fragmented by functional or hierarchical boundaries. These barriers can keep groups from integrating unique expertise and thus decrease quality, efficiency, and innovation.

- *Promoting Innovation Through Connectivity in New-Product Development or Process Improvement Initiatives.* Most important innovation is a collaborative endeavor, both in conception and implementation. Whether focused on new-product development or process improvement initiatives, network analysis can be particularly important for revealing how a team is integrating its expertise and how effectively it is drawing on the expertise of others in the organization.

- *Facilitating Post-Merger Integration and Large-Scale Organizational Change.* Particularly in knowledge-intensive settings, large-scale change is an issue of network integration. Network analysis done before a change initiative can help inform the change as well as identify people whom a sponsor might want to engage early in the process to diffuse information about the change. Network analysis can also be done as a follow-up six to nine months after implementation. Often these assessments reveal issues that leaders are unaware of but must address for the initiative to succeed.

- *Supporting Communities of Practice.* Communities of practice usually are not recognized formally but can be critical to an organization's ability to leverage functional expertise that is dispersed by physical location or organizational design. Managers can use network analysis both to uncover key members of the community and to assess connectivity.

- *Forming Strategic Partnerships and Alliances.* Executives are increasingly employing cross-organizational initiatives such as alliances and other strategic partnerships to leverage unique capabilities of organizations. Network analysis can illuminate the effectiveness of such initiatives in terms of information flow, knowledge transfer, and decision making.

- *Improving Learning and Decision Making in Top Leadership Networks.* A core function of top executive teams is to acquire information, make sound decisions, and convey those decisions effectively to the broader organization. Network analysis, when done with both the top leadership team and the next layer down, can help assess not only connections within a top leadership team but also how information is entering and leaving this group.

After you have identified a strategically important network, the second key consideration is the size of the group. In theory, social network analysis can be conducted with entire organizations. In reality, you are limited by people's willingness to complete lengthy surveys. When we conduct a network analysis, we ask each person to rate his or her interactions with all other members of the group. For example, if we have a network of 100 people, we ask each person to rate relationships with the 99 other people in the network. To ensure a high survey response rate, we tend to limit the number of people we assess to about 250.

Other techniques, such as mining e-mail communications, can reduce the burden on respondents and support analysis of larger groups. However, this approach often results in a less precise understanding of the relationships. As a result, we tend to assess large networks by focusing on a subgroup in which collaboration is critical. For example, if we are interested in networks across core processes or across divisions of a conglomerate, we might pick a certain hierarchical level where collaboration should be occurring. Alternatively, in merger or alliance scenarios, we might not consider the full population of each company but only a list of people from each organization who should be collaborating in light of strategic objectives.

Step 2: Assess Meaningful and Actionable Relationships

After you have identified a strategically important group, the second step in a social network analysis is to collect information you need to map the relationships. The relationships must meaningfully reveal a group's inner workings, and they must be actionable for managers after the results are disclosed. Often the communication network alone does not provide enough detail, so we push executives to consider more precise kinds of relationships. Table A-1 outlines several relationships that we, and many others, have found helpful.

Most companies are keenly interested in work-related collaboration, so we almost always map information flow. When possible, we also check both parties' perception of the relationship. For example, we might ask Bob whether he goes to Ann for information and then ask

TABLE A-1

Questions to Uncover Important Network Relationships

Relationships That Reveal Collaboration in a Network. The communication and the information relationship can be strong indicators of current or recent collaboration within a network. The problem-solving and innovation relationships tend to be more selective and require a higher level of trust between people. Assessing some combination of these relationships is often important because they characterize how work is getting done in knowledge-intensive settings.

Communication	• How often do you talk with the following people regarding <topic x>? • How much do you typically communicate with each person relative to others in the group?
Information	• How frequently have you acquired information necessary to do your work from this person in the past three months? • Please indicate the extent to which each person provides you with information you use to accomplish your work. • From whom do you typically seek work-related information? • To whom do you typically give work-related information?
Problem solving	• Whom do you typically turn to for help in thinking through a new or challenging problem at work? • How effective is each person in helping you to think through new or challenging problems at work?
Innovation	• Whom are you likely to turn to in order to discuss a new or innovative idea?

(continued)

TABLE A-1 *(continued)*

Relationships That Reveal the Information-Sharing Potential of a Network. Assessing these relationships, either individually or by combining them, can provide actionable ways of improving a network's potential to react to new opportunities and threats (covered in chapter 3).

Knowledge awareness	• I understand this person's knowledge and skills. This does not necessarily mean that I have these skills or am knowledgeable in these domains but that I understand what skills this person has and the domains he or she is knowledgeable in.
Access	• When I need information or advice, this person is generally accessible to me within a sufficient amount of time to help me solve my problem.
Engagement	• If I ask this person for help, I can feel confident that he or she will actively engage in problem solving with me.
Safety	• Please indicate the extent to which you feel personally comfortable asking this person for information or advice on work-related topics.

Relationships That Reveal Rigidity in a Network. These relationships highlight constraints in a network, such as bottlenecks, due to overdependence on a key decision maker or clustering around powerful personalities.

Decision making	• Please indicate whom you turn to for input prior to making an important decision.
Communicate more	• I would be more effective in my work if I were able to communicate more with this person.
Task flow	• Please indicate the extent to which people listed below provide you with inputs necessary to do your job.
	• Please indicate the extent to which you distribute outputs from your work to the people listed below.
Power or influence	• Please indicate the extent to which you consider each person listed below to be influential at [the name of the organization]—that is, people who seem to have pull, weight, or clout in this company.

Relationships That Reveal Well-Being and Supportiveness in a Network. These dimensions of relationships can be used in various combinations to assess the general atmosphere and supportiveness within a group.

Liking	• Please indicate how much you like each person.
Friendship	• Please indicate the people you consider to be personal friends, that is, those people you see most frequently for informal activities such as going out to lunch, dinner, drinks, visiting one another's homes, and so on.
Career support	• Please indicate who has contributed to your professional growth and development. Include people who have taken an active interest in and helped to advance your career.
Personal support	• Please indicate people you turn to for personal support when your work is going poorly, a project is failing, or you are frustrated with certain decisions.
Energy	• When you interact with this person, how does it affect your energy level?
Trust	• Please indicate the people in this group you would trust to keep your best interests in mind.

Ann whether Bob comes to her for information. Assessing both perspectives provides a more accurate view of the network. It can also help us determine when people attempt to inflate their importance in a network by claiming to collaborate with everyone (yet others don't acknowledge this). In addition, we often go beyond simple information networks to look at deeper relationships, such as problem solving, or specific kinds of knowledge that must circulate for the group to be successful.

As discussed in chapter 3, we also typically map sets of relationships that reveal a network's potential to respond to new opportunities or projects. When we map information, communication, or problem-solving networks, we see who is currently collaborating or has recently interacted. Although this information is interesting, it does not tell us about a group's ability to reach out to others when new projects or opportunities come along. As a result, we often map dimensions of relationships that predict whom people are able to seek out when new problems arise (even though they might not currently be getting information from these people) as well as dimensions that improve the quality of the interaction itself. We call this a latent network view because it discloses a group that could be leveraged in the future.

Relationship questions can also be effective for discovering rigidities in a network. For example, we have mapped networks of decision making or work flow to get a sense of how hierarchy or job design might be overloading a network. And networks can be powerful indicators of the atmosphere in an organization. For example, we might map networks of career or personal support, trust, or energy because these dimensions matter for quality of work life as well as information flow and learning.

In short, the ability to map networks of relationships is limitless. The key is to pick relationships that address challenges or strategic imperatives of the group and that are actionable once you find areas to target for improvement. Although we have used all the questions in table A-1 on numerous occasions, we consistently rely on three questions (and various combinations) because of the opportunities for improvement that emerge from these views: information you need to do your work, awareness of someone's knowledge and skills, and the people with whom you would like to communicate more. Figure A-1 shows a typical social network analysis survey using these three questions. The survey also includes demographic questions about an individual's location, department, and so on, as well as a set of questions on an individual's personal network.

Example Survey

Social Network Analysis Survey

Feedback I am receiving indicates that we all feel a need to communicate better and more effectively among ourselves and with other groups. We're hoping that doing some "baseline" analysis utilizing social network analysis will help us figure out what we could do to improve, especially in regard to cross-functional collaboration. I'm asking that you take the time to provide your input on the attached spreadsheet, and send the completed spreadsheet to jsmith@.xyzcompany.com for analysis (preferably by November 10th, but sooner is better; to make processing easier, please rename the spreadsheet before sending it back, e.g., to your last name). Hopefully, this shouldn't take you more than 20 minutes to complete. In order to be most effective, we need very high "participation" from those who have been asked to participate.

Please note that your answers are confidential. Results that identify you by name will be kept within the team administering this questionnaire. Outside of that group, we will only release aggregated data that will not identify you by name.

I'm looking forward to seeing what we can learn.

Thanks!
Jane Smith, VP for Human Resources

Please provide the following information about yourself:

Name

Tenure in Organization (in months)

Hierarchical Level

Location

Department

Primary Function

Please identify up to twenty people (Note: we provided only eight lines below for space considerations) who are important in terms of providing you with information to do your work or helping you think about complex problems posed by your work. These may or may not be people you communicate with on a regular basis and can come from within the organization or outside (e.g., clients, associates in other offices, colleagues in other organizations, friends, family, etc.).

Name
1
2
3
4
5
6
7
8

For each of the people who you chose above, please answer the following four questions.

Q1. What is each person's physical proximity to you?

1 = same floor
2 = different floor
3 = different building
4 = different city
5 = different country

Q2. Please indicate the organization in which each person works.

1 = within same department
2 = outside department, inside business unit
3 = outside business unit, inside organization
4 = outside organization

Q3. How long have you known each person?

1 = less than 1 year
2 = 1–3 years
3 = 3–5 years
4 = 5–10 years
5 = 10+ years

Q4. Please indicate each person's hierarchical level within the organization relative to your own.

1 = higher than yours
2 = equal to yours
3 = lower than yours
4 = not applicable

Name	Question 1	Question 2	Question 3	Question 4
1.				
2.				
3.				
4.				
5.				
6.				
7.				
8.				

(continued)

FIGURE A-1 *(continued)*

Below are three network questions. To the right of each question is the response scale to use in answering the question. If you do not know an individual listed in the questionnaire, leave your answer blank; if you know the person, select the appropriate response from 1 to 5.

Q1: Information—Please indicate the frequency with which you typically turn to each person below for information on work-related topics.

0 = I Do Not Know This Person	3 = Sometimes
1 = Never	4 = Often
2 = Seldom	5 = Very Often

Q2: Awareness—I understand this person's skills and knowledge. This does not necessarily mean that I have these skills or that I am knowledgeable in these domains, but that I understand what skills this person has and what domains they are knowledgeable in.

0 = I Do Not Know This Person	3 = Neutral
1 = Strongly Disagree	4 = Agree
2 = Disagree	5 = Strongly Agree

Q3: Communicate More—I would be more effective in my work if I were able to communicate with this person more.

0 = I Do Not Know This Person	3 = Neutral
1 = Strongly Disagree	4 = Agree
2 = Disagree	5 = Strongly Agree

	Q1 Information	Q2 Awareness	Q3 Communicate More
London			
1. Smith, David			
2. Brown, Anne			
3. Chen, Paul			
4. Black, Susan			
5. Davis, Alan			
6. Jones, Chris			
New York			
7. Cox, Robert			
8. Elliot, John			
9. Daniels, Brian			
10. Peters, Erin			
Chicago			
11. Cohen, Bob			
12. Parker, Dave			

Note: This is only a template of many possible kinds of questions and response scales that could be employed. Readers should customize this for use in their own organizations.

Beyond choosing meaningful and actionable relationships, effective network analyses also require a high response rate. Missing a key person can have a profound impact on your understanding of the network. There are various ways of improving the survey response rate, such as individualized or small-group follow-up e-mails and phone calls. Some organizations have offered gifts to encourage participation. For example, an oil and gas organization we worked with gave company pens to each person who participated. Once word spread that each respondent was to receive a gift, the number of survey responses jumped dramatically. Other organizations appoint a few ambassadors of the effort, who then follow up with those they know in the network to ensure a high response rate. In general, when the project has the appropriate level of sponsorship, obtaining a good response rate is not difficult.

A final critical issue in survey design lies in establishing confidentiality. Network diagrams identifying people's names and relationships can be highly revealing. We find that people are very interested in understanding patterns of information flow within a group. Going deeper than this and considering relationships such as trust can be much more inflammatory. An organization's willingness to explore network issues seems to reflect its culture. Some organizations are enthusiastic about seeing who is energized by whom and what can be done to promote energy levels. Others are reluctant to consider even work-related information. It is critical early on to establish guarantees to employees regarding the confidentiality of the data and then ensure that this commitment is adhered to.

We typically take one of three approaches to confidentiality. The first is full disclosure of the results via an all-employee debriefing or other communication. Often we give a presentation in which we describe the network approach and results, and then indicate that we would like to engage with this group to help promote collaboration. At this point we give out our e-mail addresses and indicate that we would like to share results with the group by identifying the names of people in the networks; however, we do not want anyone to be uncomfortable with this approach. We then tell people to e-mail us within a week if they are uncomfortable, and we also tell them that if we get *even one* e-mail (which we will hold in confidence), we will not disclose names.

A second approach is to allow only one person or a select group to see the full results so that helpful action can be taken. It might be the leader of a group, or it might be an informal committee of three to four people interested in helping promote connectivity in the group. In such cases, we disclose in the survey instructions the people who will see the network information.

A third approach is to disclose no names whatsoever, an option that yields more pragmatic information than you might think at first blush. Although enthusiasm in a debriefing session is always higher when names are disclosed, you can do a tremendous amount with network analysis without revealing people's identities. For example, you can use different-shaped nodes in the network to show splits across locations, hierarchy, or domains of expertise. Several other kinds of analyses can be conducted that provide meaningful feedback to a group and can engage them in generating solutions without disclosing names.

Step 3: Visually Analyze the Results

Once the data have been collected, you can analyze it using a network software package. A variety of packages are available. Some of them combine drawing functionality with quantitative analysis, and others specialize in one or the other. For a comprehensive list of software packages, see the International Network for Social Network Analysis Web site at <http://www.sfu.ca/~insna/>. The examples in this book, as well as much of the analysis we have conducted over the past several years, have been done using a combination of UCINET, NetDraw, and Pajek. Another software package commonly used by businesspeople is Inflow.

How do you interpret network pictures? We will start with a couple of basic concepts. First, a line between two people on a network diagram indicates a relationship between them. For example, figure A-2 illustrates a network in which we asked, "Whom do you typically turn to for information to help you do your job?" Here, a line between people indicates an information-seeking relationship. Lines in network diagrams obviously mean different things depending on the questions asked.

Second, the arrowheads represent the direction of the relationship. For example, in figure A-2, an arrowhead pointing from Joe to Sue indicates that Joe is seeking information from Sue. In this example, there is not an arrowhead pointing the other way, and this indicates that Sue does not seek information from Joe; the relationship is not reciprocal.

Directionality in relationships can indicate very different things about network participants. Someone attracting a lot of arrows might

FIGURE A-2

A Typical Social Network Diagram

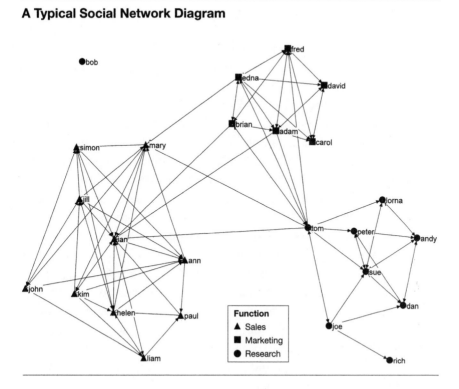

be an expert you do not want to lose (or potentially might be a bottle-neck). Someone with a lot of arrows radiating out might be a drain on other people's time (or might be in an administrative role that requires obtaining information from others).

The network software drawing packages use a step-by-step mathematical process to draw the network diagram. The algorithms usually place the people with the most ties in the center of the network and those with the fewest ties on the outside. The software also groups people with like ties together as well as applies numerous other criteria such as trying to equalize the length of the lines between people. Each person represented in the network can be assigned a shape to represent a meaningful characteristic. For example, in figure A-2 the people have been coded by three functions: research, sales, and marketing. You can add further detail by changing the size of the circles to signify other demographic characteristics. For example, you could make all managers big circles and all nonmanagers small circles. The length of a line does not mean anything, but you can vary the width to illustrate the strength or frequency of a relationship. In general, although visualization options can be useful, they should be used sparingly to avoid information overload and confusion in workshops.

When we share this information with managers, we typically highlight central and peripheral people and then subgroups in the network. Central people might be experts or bottlenecks (only follow-up interviews can tell for certain) and are clearly distinguished by the number of relationships they have and often (though not always) by being positioned at the center of the network by the drawing algorithm. For example, in figure A-2, Ian (in the center of the group on the left) is one of the central people in the network. You can also find peripheral people, such as Rich, who have few arrowheads directed to them. A special case of a peripheral person is Bob, who has no connections to anyone and is isolated from the group. It is important to identify peripheral people because they are often underutilized resources and are more likely to leave an organization than their better-connected colleagues.

Network diagrams also allow you to find out whether the network is split into subgroups. Subgroups can occur when there are impediments to the relationships between people; impediments can include political tensions, incentives, and physical distance, to name a few. When demographic information is analyzed in conjunction with the network diagram, it is possible to tell whether the subgroup has an identifying characteristic, such as location, function, hierarchy, tenure, age, or gender. In figure A-2, the network is split into the three functions.

Such splits may be the most efficient way of working if little information sharing is necessary between groups. But splits may also be detrimental. When you're trying to improve connectivity, it's important to know where the splits are and to understand the reasons for them.

Step 4: Quantitatively Analyze the Results

Quantitative analysis is especially important for large networks. For example, it is not always possible to pinpoint the most central people in a network that has multiple subgroups or many people. Typical quantitative analyses look at both the group as a whole and at how people are embedded in the network. You can conduct literally hundreds of types of analyses. In the networks that we have analyzed, we have looked at many of the available measures and have shared the results with managers to see which approaches were most helpful. Table A-2 gives a brief overview of the network measures that we have found most useful in terms of providing managers with actionable information.[2] This is by no means a full listing of analytic approaches. If you are interested in greater depth on analytic issues, Stanley Wasserman and Katherine Faust's *Social Network Analysis* provides a more comprehensive set of measures.

In terms of people's positions in a network, an important measure is *degree centrality*, which reflects the number of direct connections a person has. It provides a view of the people who are over- and underextended and can be considered in terms of both incoming and outgoing connections. For example, in figure A-2 the person with the highest degree measure is Ian, whom eleven people go to for information. The network may be overly dependent on him. The person with the lowest measure is Bob, to whom no one goes for information. He may be an underutilized resource and most likely feels isolated from the group.

TABLE A-2

Actionable Network Metrics

Individual Measures

In-degree centrality	The number of incoming ties a person has for a given relationship (such as communication or trust).
Out-degree centrality	The number of outgoing ties a person has for a given relationship (such as communication or trust).
Betweenness centrality	The extent to which a particular person lies "between" the various other people in the network. Networks that contain individuals with high betweenness are vulnerable to having information flows disrupted by power plays or key individuals leaving.
Closeness centrality	The extent to which a person lies at short distances to many other people in the network. On average, persons highly central with respect to closeness tend to hear information sooner than others.
Brokerage measures	We tend to focus on four measures here: people who broker connections within the same group (coordinators); those who broker connections between their own group and another (representatives and gatekeepers); and those who broker connections between two different groups (liaisons).

Group Measures

Density	The number of individuals who have a given type of tie with each other, expressed as a percentage of the maximum possible.
Cohesion	The average of the shortest paths between every pair of people in the network.

You can also analyze degree centrality by comparing the number of incoming connections with the number of outgoing ones in a scatter plot. This indicates three important points about the roles people play in the network. First, you can visualize the major sources and seekers of information. If you find people who have a high number of information-seeking ties but few people going to them for information when they are supposed to be experts, then things are not working as anticipated. If the reverse is true, it could also be a cause for concern.

Second, if you find that the group is heavily reliant on one person for information, it might make sense to give this person time to play a subject-matter expert role or to reallocate tasks assigned to him or her. Third, those with low numbers of incoming and outgoing ties are clearly isolated from the group. For part-time employees or high-end experts, living on the periphery is just fine. But for others this might not be the case, and there are targeted actions managers can take to help integrate them.

It can also be useful to compare people's centrality scores in two different networks. For example, we often compare the centrality scores of the information network with those of the "communicate more" network. Typically we find that leaders or experts end up being *both* the most sought-after person *and* the person with whom most people want to communicate more. For example, we have found leaders or experts who had more than fifty people relying on them for information and another fifty who wanted more of their time. Obviously, there are limits to any one person's ability to support a group in these situations. Thus, as described in this book, we often focus on reallocating decision rights and information domains to alleviate the overly consumed as well as draw in more peripheral members.

Comparing centrality scores for the information and "communicate more" networks also helps identify peripheral people or groups. Those with low information scores are isolated from the group, and if few people want to communicate more with them they are unlikely to become integrated without assistance. In other scenarios, we might find that one division does not seek information from another *and* has no desire to communicate more with that division. If collaboration at that network juncture is important to the organization, then a change is needed. Rather than simply provide an opportunity to collaborate through a technology tool or a face-to-face forum, leaders must convince each division of the importance of working together.

For sharing actionable information with managers, we have found the full network measures of density and cohesion helpful. *Network density* looks at the level of connectivity within the entire network and is defined, using percentages, as the actual number of ties divided by the total number of possible ties. In this measure, if each person were connected to every other person in the network, density would be 100 percent; if there were no connections, network density would be 0 percent. This figure is affected by the group's size; it is much easier for ten people to be fully connected than one hundred. When you interpret network density, you must either relate groups of similar size or determine an ideal network pattern depending on the objectives of the group.

One useful analysis that uses network density is to divide people into subgroups—by, for example, function or location—and calculate network density figures within and between subgroups. Then you create a density table such as the one in table A-3. The percentages down the diagonal in table A-3 are the within-function network density scores. For example, of all possible connections within the marketing function, 83 percent exist. If you look back at figure A-2, you can see that almost all the people in marketing are connected to one another.

The off-diagonal percentages indicate the between-group network density scores. For example, the network density figure for the connections between marketing and sales is 5 percent, indicating very few connections: only three, according to figure A-2. You would not expect all the subgroups to have a high level of connection with each other, but this measure allows you to find out whether the groups that you believe should be connected actually are. For example, in the network in figure A-2 you might expect there to be a high level of connection between sales and marketing but not necessarily as many connections between

TABLE A-3

Density Table

	To:		
FROM:	Marketing	Sales	Research
Marketing	83%	5%	6%
Sales	0%	46%	0%
Research	6%	2%	38%

research and sales. Again, though, as with overall density, a network analyst must always bear in mind that these percentages are affected by subgroup size.

Another useful group measure, *cohesion*, is based on the shortest path—in other words, the minimum number of links to get from one person to another—between every possible pair in the network. The cohesion score for the entire network is the average of all the possible scores between the various pairs of people. For example, in figure A-2 the shortest number of links from Tom to Rich is two, whereas from Joe to Kim it is three. If we took the average for the entire network we would find that the cohesion score for this network is 2.2. Ideally, we would like the average cohesion score to be around 2 in groups where managers are interested in employees leveraging each other's expertise. Consider your own behavior. You are sure to call a friend for information and likely to call someone the friend refers you to; after that, however, the odds of continuing your search using referrals diminishes rapidly (as does the likelihood that a stranger will respond).

In short, we could have come up with insights about key individuals as well as the network as a whole just by analyzing the network picture in figure A-2, but it is also important to look at it quantitatively. Why? First, visually assessing networks as they grow beyond forty or so people can be challenging. The diagrams appear cluttered, so it is important to focus on subgroups and quantitative analysis to get an accurate view. Second, as the diagrams become more complex, it seems that people pick out patterns based on their beliefs as opposed to what the network information reveals, and they thereby miss or misinterpret important points. Quantitative techniques, such as the ones we have described here, help reduce bias in network interpretation.

Step 5: Create Meaningful Feedback Sessions

Although network analysis is an extremely useful way to understand the relationships between people in a particular group, it does not necessarily reveal why certain relationships are present or absent, or even what is effective or ineffective in a group. To get a better understanding of the dynamics behind the network, we conduct interviews with a select number of people, usually about eight to ten network members. We try to use the network analysis to determine which people to interview. For example, we normally interview people who are playing central and peripheral roles in the network. To get a variety of perspectives, we also try to interview people from each of the hierarchical levels as well as those new to the group and those who have a longer tenure.

Reporting methods can vary from a written document to workshops with all the network participants. We prefer the latter approach and have worked with groups of more than a hundred people in very productive workshops.

Such sessions typically include two parts. First, we present an overview of network analysis to orient the participants, and then we provide a summary presentation of ten or so slides highlighting important points from the analysis. This part of the workshop is focused on generating agreement on important issues for that group. Because network analysis is often new to people, the diagrams generate a great deal of energy and enthusiasm. In the second half of these workshops, the participants form smaller groups and brainstorm ways to promote appropriate connectivity and ensure that organizational context will not push the network back to ineffective patterns. These subgroups then debrief the larger group, and ideas are cataloged for action planning.

In both stages, we focus on what can be done to improve the effectiveness of the group. Rather than question why someone or some department is peripheral or central, it is more constructive to focus on how the organization can overcome unproductive patterns. Furthermore, we don't present results as much as we use the information to help define, along with members of the group, important issues and action items. By virtue of this process, we tend to get agreement on important issues to address and next steps to take. Conducted in the way we describe, the workshops are both diagnostic and a first step in a change management program.

Step 6: Assess Progress and Effectiveness

Conducting a network analysis of a group indicates the level of connectivity only at a certain point in time. Repeating this process after six to nine months can reveal whether there has been a change in the network. This follow-up is especially important if you are trying to understand the effect of a specific managerial action. Network analysis allows you to visualize the effect of changes that traditionally are hard to measure, such as implementation of a collaborative technology or certain organizational development initiatives.

We also track objective measures of performance over time. This is particularly important because of the potential for biased survey responses the second time around. Astute respondents, knowing what is coming, may artificially inflate their responses to make themselves look more important than they are. In fact, in one organization we heard that someone was lobbying others to give her higher ratings in the survey. We can correct for this in part by assessing both sides of the relationship, as described earlier. But we also track other measures appropriate to the group to be sure that we are having the desired impact on business performance.

Case Example: A Network Analysis

We worked with an oil and gas services organization that was drawn to the social network analysis methodology because of its ability to give an objective snapshot of how knowledge and information flowed. One of the most critical business challenges this company faced was to reduce the cost of poor quality at on-shore and off-shore well sites around the world. Poor quality damaged not only short-term financial results but also long-term credibility. In this competitive industry, the company's services were often viewed as a commodity. If the organization did not execute flawlessly and efficiently, it would not retain valued customers.

Step 1: Identifying a Strategically Important Group

We conducted a network analysis of a customer-facing service group. These employees worked with large oil companies to set up well sites for production all around the world. For example, the group did the highly specialized work of packing sand around a well pipe to set it in place to withstand the stress and rigor of a production environment. Because of differences in environmental conditions at the various sites, there was some variance in the techniques used, but there were many similarities in the broad problems faced. Despite these commonalities, the same problems were often solved several times over in different parts of the world, and relevant expertise in the organization was often not located in a timely manner. Both of these issues resulted in poor quality and inefficient work. Because the group was large, we selected approximately one hundred people from the seven countries that were the most strategically important in terms of quality of service.

The company wanted to conduct the network analysis for two reasons. First, senior managers wanted to understand the network of connections among the different countries. They believed that promoting collaboration across sites would reduce rework as well as improve the quality and innovativeness of the work done on each project. Second, the customer service group in one of the countries had achieved substantial reductions in losses related to poor quality. Management was keenly interested in learning whether this correlated with the level of collaboration among functional groups in that country.

Step 2: Assessing Meaningful and Actionable Relationships

In consultation with the managers of the group, we decided to do a combined personal network and group network survey to assess the relationships both within and outside this group. Managers were particularly interested in the number of connections people had with field personnel and the technology center. We asked three group, or bounded, network questions in the survey. First, we asked each respondent, "Who provides you with information to do your work?" to find out the level of information sharing within and between the regions. Second, we asked the respondents to indicate their "awareness of the knowledge and skills" of each person in the group to understand whether employees were sufficiently aware of and able to tap into the expertise of those outside their own region. Finally, we asked respondents to indicate the "effect on [their] energy level of interacting with person X" to understand energy flow and likelihood of innovation within the network.

Step 3: Visually Analyzing the Results

As figure A-3 shows, the network maps revealed that there was very little information sharing across countries. In many cases there were only four or five connections between two countries, and in some cases no connections at all. On a more positive note, we did find a high level of collaboration within each country. This was especially the case in the country that had successfully reduced losses due to poor quality. A close look at this country indicated that there was a high level of collaboration between the functional groups.

FIGURE A-3

Information Network of a Product and Services Group

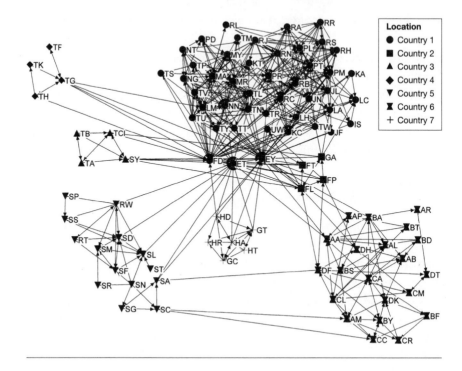

It is also clear from the network map in figure A-3 that three people were playing prominent boundary-spanning roles between several of the countries. In fact, when we removed these three people (FD, ET, and EY) from the network, we found that there were fewer than fifteen connections remaining between countries. Our initial belief was that these boundary spanners were acting as vital conduits of information between the countries. To our surprise, after interviewing several key people, we found that the boundary spanners, known as global advisers, were acting more as information bottlenecks than connection facilitators.

These roles had been created in an organizational redesign in the early 1990s as part of an initiative to improve quality and accountability. The initial impact of these advisers had been positive for service quality, but over time, more employees were seeking these people out and the network had become far too dependent on them. The global advisers were called on to make even the most trivial decisions, and they were repeatedly asked basic questions, such as about replacement part numbers. When we interviewed the three advisers, they agreed that up to 80 percent of the decisions they were being asked to make could be made by others.

Careful analysis of the knowledge and skills awareness network indicated that the main reason people were not sharing information across countries was that they were not aware of each other's knowledge and skills. Many of those whom we interviewed agreed that without any explicit way to identify expertise, only a "knowledge accident" would lead to any type of collaboration. This lack of awareness was further complicated by a lack of trust between people in different countries. In this organization, people needed to have worked side-by-side to establish the trust necessary for collaboration.

Step 4: Quantitatively Analyzing the Results

Quantitative analysis confirmed our findings from the visual analysis. For example, the percentages of connectivity down the diagonal in table A-4 clearly showed that there was a high level of collaboration within each country. In contrast, the off-diagonal percentages indicated that there was almost no collaboration between the countries. The density and cohesion metrics for the network as a whole also indicated that there was a low overall level of collaboration within the group. In addition, the quantitative analysis confirmed the boundary-spanning roles played by FD, ET, and EY.

TABLE A-4

Collaboration Within and Between Countries

	To:						
FROM:	Country 1	Country 2	Country 3	Country 4	Country 5	Country 6	Country 7
Country 1	50%	3%	0%	19%	0%	5%	16%
Country 2	3%	100%	0%	0%	0%	0%	6%
Country 3	0%	0%	42%	0%	0%	2%	2%
Country 4	25%	0%	0%	75%	0%	0%	9%
Country 5	0%	0%	0%	0%	77%	2%	4%
Country 6	6%	1%	1%	0%	2%	45%	1%
Country 7	11%	4%	0%	2%	1%	1%	38%

Step 5: Creating Meaningful Feedback Sessions

Once completed, the network analysis was shared with many of the participants in the survey as well as some key stakeholders in the organization. We conducted a facilitated half-day session with many network members, and it was deemed a resounding success on two fronts. First, participants made numerous positive suggestions about how to improve connectivity in the network. Second, the session brought together many people who had previously not known each other.

Step 6: Assessing Progress and Effectiveness

As a result of the network analysis, the interviews, the feedback session, and a prior commitment to improve collaboration, the organization made several changes. First, it developed a business-driven communication plan, which provided a clear charter to tackle tangible initiatives. Second, the company developed a self-service Web portal that included expert locator functionality. This was driven and fortified by knowledge brokers, whose role was to maintain and update expertise profiles while they forwarded open issues to experts without waiting for these experts to see issues generated. This initiative helped solve problems in much less time than before the community was in place.

Third, several community of practice events were conducted. These events helped community members meet and get to know each other, enhancing trust and therefore facilitating sharing and the breaking down of barriers. Fourth, to address the role of the three people who had become bottlenecks, specific people in each of the countries were assigned the role of local knowledge champions. Their task was to identify local subject-matter experts, actively encourage information sharing within each country, and broker connections between people in different countries. This signaled a move away from a centralized organization model to one that was more dispersed and participatory, with an emphasis on distributed decision making.

Appendix B

Tools for Promoting
Network Connectivity

THIS APPENDIX provides three kinds of tools for promoting network connectivity. The first is a self-assessment that helps individuals better understand their personal networks. The second is a set of facilitation exercises that improve connectivity within networks through relationship building. The third is a diagnostic to ascertain how organizational context affects informal networks.

Assessment 1: Personal Network Diagnostic

This diagnostic (see figure B-1) allows you to better understand your personal network and create an action plan to optimize its effectiveness. You can find an electronic version of this on Rob Cross's personal Web site (<www.robcross.org>) if you're interested in an automated version of this process that can quickly generate very detailed feedback and network-building suggestions.

The first step is to indicate whom you turn to for information to do your work. The second step is to define the characteristics of these relationships, information that feeds into step 3, identifying any biases in your network. For example, are you likely to turn only to people in your own location or function, or do you go to people throughout the organization for information to help you do your work? By identifying the biases in your network, you can create an action plan to address areas in your network where you are overinvested and areas where you are underinvested. The fourth step is to itemize the types of expertise you need to do your work, and in step 5 you can relate these needs to your network. This enables you to determine expertise gaps or excessive reliance on one or two people (step 6).

FIGURE B-1a

A Brief Personal Network Assessment: Step 1

Step 1: Write down the names of people you rely on for information or problem solving to do your work. These people can come from any and all walks of life.

Names

A Brief Personal Network Assessment: Step 2

Step 2: List the number of relationships that fall into each category for the major descriptors below.

	Group
1 = within same group	
2 = outside group, within same business unit	
3 = outside business unit, within same division	
4 = outside division, within same organization	
5 = different organization	

	Proximity
1 = works immediately next to me	
2 = same floor	
3 = different floor	
4 = different building	
5 = different city	
6 = different country	

	Interaction
1 = never	
2 = seldom	
3 = sometimes	
4 = frequently	
5 = very frequently	

	Effort
1 = 1 hour or less per month	
2 = 2–3 hours per month	
3 = 1 hour per week	
4 = 2–3 hours per week	
5 = 1 hour or more per day	

	Time Known
1 = less than 1 year	
2 = 1–3 years	
3 = 3–5 years	
4 = 5–10 years	
5 = 10+ years	

	Hierarchy
1 = higher than yours	
2 = equal to yours	
3 = lower than yours	
4 = not applicable	

	Primary Medium
1 = unplanned face-to-face meetings	
2 = planned face-to-face meetings	
3 = telephone	
4 = e-mail	
5 = instant messaging	

	Gender
1 = same	
2 = different	

	Age
1 = younger by 6 years or more	
2 = your age plus or minus 5 years	
3 = older by more than 6 years	

	Ethnicity
1 = same ethnicity	
2 = different ethnicity	

A Brief Personal Network Assessment: Step 3

Step 3: Take a look at the composition of your network and identify biases that may affect how you do your job. For example, do you have a tendency to go only to people who are accessible to you rather than to those who may have more relevant information? Note implications these biases have for the way you do your work and actions you can take to resolve these issues.

Bias	Implication/Action

A Brief Personal Network Assessment: Step 4

Step 4: Identify up to eight skills or types of expertise necessary for you to do your job. For example, types of expertise can be technical such as programming skills, administrative such as knowledge of company-specific databases and software, or managerial such as program management or leadership skills.

Expertise you need to do your work
1.
2.
3.
4.
5.
6.
7.
8.

FIGURE B-1e

A Brief Personal Network Assessment: Step 5

Step 5: Transfer the types of expertise to the first row and the people in your personal network to the first column of the table below. (The number of rows can be expanded as appropriate.) Then indicate with a check mark which people you go to for which types of expertise in each of the rows. Finally, tally the number of check marks across each row and down each column.

Name	Exp. 1	Exp. 2	Exp. 3	Exp. 4	Exp. 5	Exp. 6	Exp. 7	Exp. 8	Total
1.									
2.									
3.									
4.									
5.									
6.									
7.									
8.									
9.									
10.									
Total									

FIGURE B-1f

A Brief Personal Network Assessment: Step 6

Step 6: Review the scores in step 5 for each of the people in your expertise network to see if there are people you are overly dependent on or people you do not leverage sufficiently (or possibly leverage for the wrong kinds of tasks). Next, review the scores for each type of expertise. Are there types of expertise you need to further develop but do not have a set of relationships to help on this front? Finally, note implications of the expertise gaps and overdependencies to the way you do your work. Indicate what actions you can take to resolve these issues.

Expertise Gap/Overdependency	Implication/Action

Assessment 2: Relationship Building

These facilitated exercises help promote network connectivity through relationship building. They are split into three types. The first type is aimed at helping people to initiate relationships, the second at developing relationships, and the third at correcting and maintaining existing relationships.

There are two exercises of each type. Each exercise contains an overview, details of the materials needed, the process necessary to conduct the exercise, and the potential benefits of the exercise.

Exercises to Initiate Relationships

The Decades Exercise

This exercise is useful for new and existing groups who want to develop awareness of other people's professional expertise and personal backgrounds. At the end of the Decades exercise, each participant should have an understanding of the others' professional and personal life stories.

Materials

- Butcher-block paper

- Markers

- Flipchart

Process

1. Mount butcher-block paper to a wall. On the paper, create sections labeled by decades (1960s, 1970s, etc.) or another meaningful unit of time, leaving one section open for the future.

2. Ask each person to write or draw one event from his or her personal or professional life for each decade on the wall. In the "future" section, ask people to write down some of their goals for the next decade. Goals should be aimed at building an understanding of both personal and professional aspects of relationships, so it is important to instruct respondents to report on both dimensions.

3. Allow about twenty minutes for people to write or draw events.

4. After everyone has finished, reconvene the group. Ask each person to tell the stories that go along with the events. Allow about three to seven minutes per person.

5. After each person has had a chance to speak, discuss as a group what you have heard. Record some key points on a flipchart.

   - What did people learn about one another?

   - What did people have in common?

   - What was surprising?

Potential Benefits

The Decades exercise allows participants to develop relationships on a personal and a professional level. One outcome is that participants learn about others' expertise while also making people aware of their own. Based on what is uncovered about professional experiences, participants may also gain a sense of others' problem-solving skills as well as their network of contacts.

Another outcome is development of the kind of personal connections that allow a feeling of safety with others. Providing an opportunity for people to relate to one another about common life experiences (whether professional or personal) helps people connect on future issues.

Time Required

Flexible, depending on group size. Minimum time, twenty minutes.

The Mystery Group Exercise

Use this exercise to encourage interaction at larger conferences, meetings, or social events. It is particularly useful for helping newcomers break into groups of people who are already well acquainted.

Materials

- Pre-event survey and color-coded nametags

Process

1. Before the meeting or event, survey the participants regarding current or past professional interests. Ask them to provide professional background information that they are willing to share with others.

2. Before the event, identify participants who have common interests or experiences but different backgrounds. Assign these people to subgroups. For example, you could put people together who have a common interest in technology but work in different parts of the organization.

3. Create nametags of the same color for each subgroup. The nametags should show only the person's name.

4. At the event, pass out the nametags and instruct participants to find the other members of their Mystery Group. Each Mystery Group shares the same color nametags as well as a common professional interest or experience.

5. This exercise can also work for assigning people to tables at social events. In this case, attendees are seated together for meals based on some common interest or professional experience. People must speak with one another to find out why they have been grouped.

Potential Benefits

The Mystery Group exercise encourages people to initiate relationships with the specific purpose of finding out their professional interests or experiences. And because this is a low-risk situation and typically takes place in a nonwork setting, people feel at ease while talking to others.

Time Required

Depends on group size.

Exercises to Develop Relationships

Baseball Cards

Use this exercise with new or existing groups. Creating baseball-type cards for each group member is a useful exercise for developing employee profiles, which can help people learn others' capabilities. Once group members create their baseball cards, the cards can be duplicated and passed around for future reference.

FIGURE B-2

Baseball Card Template

Front Side   Back Side

Birthday (mm/dd)_____

Birthplace_____

Home city_____

E-mail_____

Phone #_____

Educational background

_____

_____

_____

Career background

_____

_____

_____

Personal achievements

_____

_____

_____

Name_____

Team_____

Position_____

Materials

- Baseball card template for each participant (see figure B-2)

- Pens for each participant

- Instant or digital camera (if available)

- Printer (if digital camera is used)

- Photocopier (if camera is available)

- Scissors (if camera is available)

- Tape (if camera is available)

Process

1. Pass out pens and baseball card templates to each participant. Ask each person to fill out the template. Allow about fifteen minutes for this.

2. After everyone has finished, ask people to come up one by one for a photo (if a digital camera is available). Encourage people to be themselves in the photo. Remind them that this photo will be used for their baseball cards. If they seem reluctant, remind them that everyone's picture will be taken.

3. Ask each person to go around the room and discuss what he or she wrote on the baseball card template. Allow about twenty minutes for this.

4. If you used a digital camera, print the digital photos while the group is discussing the cards. Photo-quality paper is not necessary, but the photos will come out better if photo-quality paper is used.

5. When you have finished printing the photos, reconvene the group. Pass out the photos, tape, and scissors to each person. Ask each person to tape the photo to the baseball card template.

6. Ask everyone to pass the cards back to you. During a break, make photocopies of the cards so that each person has a card for everyone in the group. Pass around the cards to each participant, and encourage everyone to keep them for future reference. The baseball cards can serve as a reminder about people's profiles during the meeting and afterward.

Potential Benefits

Although people learn about others' knowledge and expertise in the baseball card exercise, they also build personal connections by identifying commonalties in background, education, and families. The baseball cards also provide a quick and lasting reference point for skill and personality profiles, which can be leveraged for maintaining future contact.

Time Required

Twenty to thirty minutes depending on group size.

Scavenger Hunt

Use the scavenger hunt in new or existing group situations for people to get to know one another in a low-risk environment.

Materials

- Profile sheets for each participant

- Scavenger hunt list for each participant

- Pen or pencil for each participant

- Flipchart and marker

Process

1. Before the scavenger hunt, create a profile sheet for each participant and send it to the person to fill out (allow at least one week). The facilitator uses the profile sheet to create the scavenger hunt list. Here are some sample questions for the profile sheet:

   - Describe one major project you have worked on and key skills or expertise you developed in that effort.

   - Describe your best (or worst) experience in your job.

   - What are your hobbies?

   - What is the most exotic place you have traveled for work (or personal travel)?

2. Allow enough time before the actual meeting to cull the profile sheets. Use them to create a scavenger hunt list in which the characteristics of participants are listed anonymously.

   Sample Scavenger Hunt List

Find someone who has his or her own Web site.	X
Find someone who enjoys flying as a hobby.	X
Find someone who worked on the XXX project.	X
Find someone who fell flat on his or her face in front of the CEO.	X

3. At the time of the scavenger hunt, thank everyone for filling out the profiles. Pass out pens or pencils, along with the scavenger hunt lists. Ask each participant to find one person in the group who has one of the characteristics listed. For each characteristic,

the participant must get the signature of the person who has that characteristic.

4. Allow at least thirty minutes for this exercise. As soon as someone has gotten all the signatures for each characteristic, reconvene the group to go over the scavenger hunt list. Ask the group members what they learned about each other. Record interesting points on a flipchart.

Potential Benefits

The primary outcome of this exercise is that people learn about others' expertise and background. This is especially useful for assessing others' strengths and weaknesses—a critical process for developing effective knowledge-sharing relationships. Participants also make new acquaintances in a nonthreatening and fun setting. This exercise offers an incentive for creating personal connections.

Time Required

Twenty-five to forty-five minutes or more.

Exercises to Maintain and Correct Relationships

Reconsidering Expectations

This exercise helps participants clarify or revisit a group's overall expectations for a meeting or a project. Participants learn how to offer high-quality exchanges that meet expectations throughout the meeting or in the future. Offering high-quality exchanges, not frequent exchanges, is a critical behavior for maintaining effective learning relationships in the long term.

Materials

• Flipcharts and markers

Process

1. At the beginning of the session, ask each person to think about his or her expectations or goals for the meeting or project. Break the group into subgroups of three to four people.

2. Instruct the subgroup participants to agree on what they hope to achieve in the meeting. Subgroups should record their

answers on a flipchart and choose a spokesperson for later. Remind the group to think realistically about their goals. Allow about fifteen to twenty minutes for this work.

3. Reconvene the group. Ask the spokesperson from each sub-group to report the group's expectations for the meeting. Then ask the whole group members what they learned in the exercise. Again, encourage the group to think about what outcomes would result in high-quality interactions.

4. Keep the recorded expectations for your own use for the rest of the meeting. It is important to keep the group on target for meeting their expectations. This will help facilitate a session where people leave feeling satisfied.

Potential Benefits

One benefit of this exercise is that people leave the meeting feeling that their objectives have been met. This exercise is particularly useful for helping people understand what others consider important for quality interactions.

Time Required

Twenty minutes minimum.

Your Effect on Others

Use this exercise to help participants think about how to offer quality interactions with people they turn to for problem solving. By providing a process for specifically thinking about participants' effect on others, this exercise helps them offer more productive interactions for existing learning relationships.

Materials

• Pens or pencils for each participant

• Individual/Group Template (see figure B-3)

Process

1. Distribute pens or pencils and Individual/Group Templates to each participant.

Individual/Group Template

Name of Individual or Group

_____

Positive_____

_____

_____

Neutral_____

_____

_____

Negative_____

_____

_____

Tactics for decreasing negative effect _____

_____

_____

Name of Individual or Group

_____

Positive_____

_____

_____

Neutral_____

_____

_____

Negative_____

_____

_____

Tactics for decreasing negative effect _____

_____

_____

2. Ask the group members to create a list of all the people they might turn to for help with a problem. Instruct participants to answer the following questions:

- Is this the best person to go to for the information I need?

- How will my question(s) affect his or her workload?

- What can I bring to the interaction that would benefit this person?

- Will my question(s) have a positive or negative effect on this person? How can I minimize the negative effect?

3. Remind the group to record their answers to the last question on the template and to consider ways to make interactions with this person as productive as possible.

4. Encourage participants to use what they have written as a reminder when approaching others for help.

Potential Benefits

The primary benefit of this exercise is that participants have a structured process for considering how to provide the most productive interactions with people whose relationships they value. Our research showed that relationships that are most valued for learning typically consist of high-quality exchanges.

Time Required

Ten minutes.

Assessment 3: Organizational Context Diagnostic

The organizational context diagnostic, shown in figure B-4, can be included with network surveys to help you get a sense of how aspects of context affect collaboration throughout a network. This can often be a powerful viewpoint because people in different pockets of a network have different perspectives and needs.

The diagnostic has four sections: formal structure, work management practices, human resource practices, and leadership and cultural

Organizational Context Diagnostic

For each of the following questions, please use the two scales below. Write the numbers corresponding to your answer on the lines provided.

Effectiveness of practice in promoting collaboration

1–very ineffective
2–ineffective
3–neutral
4–effective
5–very effective
6–this practice does not exist

Potential of practice to improve collaboration

1–strongly disagree
2–disagree
3–neutral
4–agree
5–strongly agree
6–not applicable

Formal Structure	Effectiveness of practice	Potential to improve collaboration
1. People in this network are encouraged to reach out to another function for expertise without going through a formal procedure or the chain of command.	_____	_____
2. Planning processes and goals explicitly address integration of functions or divisions.	_____	_____
3. Planning processes help develop insight as to how integration of disparate expertise could differentiate the organization from competitors or provide value to customers.	_____	_____
4. There are components of the organization's budget that focus on funding or supporting projects that integrate people with different expertise or from different functions and divisions.	_____	_____
5. There are processes and procedures (or accepted cultural norms) that make it easy for one person to reach out to another hierarchical level without going through the chain of command.	_____	_____
6. People in this network know which decisions they are allowed to make and which they need to consult others on (and who those other people are).	_____	_____
7. Decision rights are effectively allocated throughout the group so that work is not excessively slowed in order to obtain approvals.	_____	_____
8. Information is effectively distributed in the group rather than people having to turn to someone at a higher level for information to get work done.	_____	_____
9. Positions of influence (or committees) in this hierarchy are spread across functions or business units to help ensure integration within and across functional boundaries.	_____	_____
10. There are specific roles (such as knowledge managers) or pieces of roles (such as modified staffing coordinators) that help people connect across physical and functional boundaries.	_____	_____
11. There are informal or formal liaison roles that establish a point of contact for communication between functions or business units within or outside of the group.	_____	_____
12. Rotational assignments help integrate this group by creating relationships across boundaries created by function or physical space.	_____	_____

13. Communities of practice are supported in a way that helps integrate networks across physical, functional, or hierarchical boundaries.   _____   _____

14. Internal initiatives, such as committee work, philanthropic efforts, recruiting, and sports, help integrate people in the network.   _____   _____

Work Management Practices	Effectiveness of practice	Potential to improve collaboration
1. The employees with the most relevant expertise (rather than just those whom a leader knows and likes) are assigned to projects when they are initiated.	_____	_____
2. Once projects are staffed, all employees are encouraged to seek out those with the most relevant expertise (either in the group or elsewhere in the organization).	_____	_____
3. Employees have enough time to seek input from others or to make themselves available to help others.	_____	_____
4. People are able to shift tasks to the people with the most expertise.	_____	_____
5. There are integrated handoffs for products and services that move through different functional areas.	_____	_____
6. The physical space in which this group is housed facilitates spontaneous communication.	_____	_____
7. A balance of synchronous and asynchronous technologies is used to support virtual work.	_____	_____
8. Skill-profiling systems exist that allow individuals to tap into expertise not already known to them.	_____	_____
9. Synchronous technologies are employed to supplement face-to-face interactions.	_____	_____
10. Asynchronous technologies are employed that allow people to query others or store work products.	_____	_____
11. Instant messaging allows for serendipitous interaction.	_____	_____

Human Resources Practices	Effectiveness of practice	Potential to improve collaboration
1. This group's recruiting process screens for people who have demonstrated collaborative behaviors.	_____	_____
2. This group's recruiting process screens for people with depth and breadth of expertise, which will make them effective integrators across disciplines.	_____	_____
3. Orientation practices help new people develop an awareness of who does what in the organization.	_____	_____
4. Orientation practices help make the group aware of the new person's expertise.	_____	_____
5. Efforts are made to conduct orientation in groups so that new people have a network right from the start.	_____	_____
6. There are activities to support new cohorts after orientation, such as ongoing training and informal get-togethers.	_____	_____

(continued)

FIGURE B-4 *(continued)*

---

7. In general, there is an effort to conduct training in a group   _____   _____
setting rather than sending individuals to customized programs.

8. Professional development plans help individuals develop their   _____   _____
personal networks.

9. Demonstration of collaborative behaviors is a meaningful com-   _____   _____
ponent of performance evaluation.

10. Performance feedback (at least in relation to collaborative   _____   _____
behaviors) is given by sources who have witnessed the behavior.

11. In general, the people who get the largest raises or bonuses are   _____   _____
rewarded on their collaborative behavior.

12. This group employs "spot" reward mechanisms for collabora-   _____   _____
tive behavior.

13. People in this group intrinsically value collaboration as a part of   _____   _____
their work.

Leadership and Culture	Effectiveness of practice	Potential to improve collaboration
1. Leaders of this group envision and structure work as a collaborative endeavor.	_____	_____
2. Leaders encourage collaboration in problem solving.	_____	_____
3. Leaders focus on involving people who might be on the periphery of networks.	_____	_____
4. Leaders help employees build their own personal networks.	_____	_____
5. Leaders are willing to share their networks.	_____	_____
6. Leaders direct people to those with relevant expertise rather than forcing people to come to them.	_____	_____
7. Leaders are quick to spot points within a network experiencing tensions.	_____	_____
8. Leaders of this group are active and effective communicators.	_____	_____
9. Face-to-face forums in this group are sufficiently frequent to allow for network development.	_____	_____
10. Face-to-face forums are done in such a way that people develop social ties and learn about the expertise of others.	_____	_____
11. Face-to-face forums are inclusive rather than the domain of a select few.	_____	_____
12. People are committed to a broad goal and set of values that help promote integration throughout the entire network.	_____	_____
13. "Stretch" goals encourage people to seek out allies, resources, and solutions across boundaries.	_____	_____
14. "Unwritten rules" do not prevent people from working across boundaries, sharing bad news with bosses, or admitting failure.	_____	_____
15. In general, this is a safe environment where people are not afraid to admit a lack of knowledge.	_____	_____
16. There are sufficient opportunities for people to develop trust in others.	_____	_____
17. People are willing to share information in a draft format rather than perfecting their work first.	_____	_____

practices. In each section people are asked to rate various organizational practices in terms of the practice's effectiveness and its potential to improve collaboration. Rarely do organizations employ the entire diagnostic; instead, managers select relevant items. By identifying areas where the organization is constraining informal networks, the diagnostic creates the basis for an action plan for organizational change.

You can include the assessment as part of a network analysis survey or incorporate it into a post–network analysis workshop. If it is included as part of the survey, the answers to the questions employed can be averaged and graphed as in figure B-5. Here we see the results of the formal structure questions. From the graph you can see that budget allocation (question 4) is the least effective practice, whereas planning processes (question 2) is the most effective. Reaching out across functions (question 1) and budget allocation (question 4) have the most potential and, interestingly, also have the most potential compared with current effectiveness. In this case, the two most effective initiatives would be to encourage people to reach out across functions and to restructure the budget allocation process so that it promotes collaboration.

Alternatively, network analysts can pick out the dimensions of context that either workshops or interviews suggest are most important to the group. This allows you to focus feedback and discussion on important elements and can be shared more concisely via a spider diagram. Figure B-6, for example, is based on sixteen dimensions of context that interviews suggested were particularly important in this organization.

FIGURE B-5

Improving Collaboration via Formal Structure

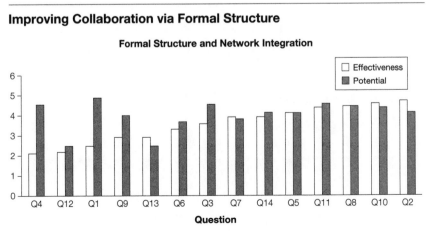

Formal Structure and Network Integration

The Effect of Predefined Context Dimensions

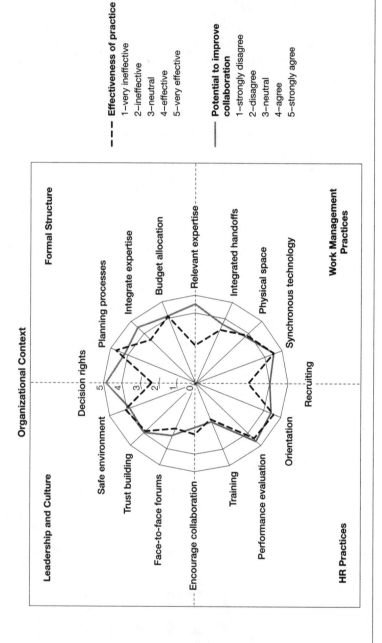

Organizational Context

Leadership and Culture

Formal Structure

Work Management Practices

HR Practices

- - - **Effectiveness of practice**
  1–very ineffective
  2–ineffective
  3–neutral
  4–effective
  5–very effective

—— **Potential to improve collaboration**
  1–strongly disagree
  2–disagree
  3–neutral
  4–agree
  5–strongly agree

If the assessment is included as part of a post–network analysis workshop, we suggest that the first half of the workshop concentrate on discussing the findings from the network analysis. In the second half, people should be divided into four subgroups, and each group should be asked to discuss one of the four sections of the checklist. Each subgroup should record its findings on a flipchart and then debrief suggestions to the entire group. You can then use voting or other approaches to generate a final action plan for the entire group.

Notes

Preface

1. W. Tsai and S. Ghoshal, "Social Capital and Value Creation: The Role of Intrafirm Networks," *Academy of Management Journal* 41, no. 4 (1998): 464–476; M. Hansen, "The Search-Transfer Problem: The Role of Weak Ties in Sharing Knowledge Across Organization Subunits," *Administrative Science Quarterly* 44 (1999): 82–111; P. Monge and N. Contractor, "Emergence of Communication Networks," in *Handbook of Organizational Communication*, 2d ed., eds. F. Jablin and L. Putnam (Thousand Oaks, CA: Sage, 2000); R. Cross, S. Borgatti, and A. Parker, "Making Invisible Work Visible: Using Social Network Analysis to Support Strategic Collaboration," *California Management Review* 44, no. 2 (2002): 25–46; R. Cross and L. Prusak, "The People Who Make Organizations Go—or Stop," *Harvard Business Review* 80, no. 6 (2002): 1–22; T. Allen, *Managing the Flow of Technology* (Cambridge, MA: MIT Press, 1977); R. Leenders and S. Gabbay, *Corporate Social Capital and Liability* (New York: Kluwer, 1999); S. Gabbay and R. Leenders, *Social Capital in Organizations* (Stamford, CT: JAI Press, 2001); N. Lin, K. S. Cook, and R. S. Burt, *Social Capital: Theory and Research* (New York: Aldine de Gruyter, 2001); and P. Monge and N. Contractor, *Theories of Communication Networks* (New York: Oxford University Press, 2003).

2. B. Uzzi, "The Sources and Consequences of Embeddedness for the Economic Performance of Organizations: The Network Effect," *American Sociological Review* 61, (1996): 674–698; B. Uzzi, "Social Structure and Competition in Interfirm Networks: The Paradox of Embeddedness," *Administrative Science Quarterly* 42 (1997): 35–67; R. Gulati, "Social Structure and Alliance Formation Patterns: A Longitudinal Analysis," *Administrative Science Quarterly* 40 (1995): 619–652; and R. Gulati, "Where Do Interorganizational Networks Come From?" *American Journal of Sociology* 104, no. 5 (1999): 1439–1493.

3. For some time, academics and managers have discussed shifts to network forms via mechanisms such as joint ventures, partnerships, strategic alliances, and R&D consortia. See, for example, R. Miles and C. Snow, "Network Organizations: New Concepts for New Forms," *California Management Review* 28 (1986): 62–73; R. Miles and C. Snow, *Fit, Failure and the Hall of Fame* (New York: Free Press, 1994); R. Miles and C. Snow, "The New Network Firm: A Spherical Structure Built on a Human Investment Policy," *Organizational Dynamics* 23, no. 4 (1995): 5–18; C. Handy, *The Age of Paradox* (Boston: Harvard Business School Press, 1994);

C. Heckscher, "Defining the Post-bureaucratic Type," in *The Post-bureaucratic Organization: New Perspectives on Organizational Change*, eds. C. Heckscher and A. Donnellon (Thousand Oaks, CA: Sage, 1994); and J. Galbraith, *Designing Organizations: An Executive Briefing on Strategy, Structure, and Process* (San Francisco: Jossey-Bass, 1995). But such work pays little attention to employee networks within organizations.

4. J. Moreno, *Who Shall Survive?* (Washington, DC: Nervous and Mental Disease Publishing Company, 1934).

5. *New York Times*, 3 April 1933: L17.

6. B. Wellman, "The Community Question: The Intimate Networks of East Yorkers," *American Journal of Sociology* 84, no. 5 (1979): 1201–1231; B. Wellman, "Different Strokes from Different Folks: Community Ties and Social Support," *American Journal of Sociology* 96, no. 3 (1990): 558–588; and B. Wellman, J. Salaff, D. Dimitrova, L. Garton, M. Gulia, and C. Haythornthwaite, "Computer Networks as Social Networks: Collaborative Work, Telework, and Virtual Community," *Annual Review of Sociology* 22 (1996): 213–238.

7. P. Blau, *Exchange and Power in Social Life* (New York: Wiley, 1964); R. M. Emerson, "Power-Dependence Relations," *American Sociological Review* 27 (1962): 31–41; K. S. Cook and R. M. Emerson, "Power, Equity and Commitment in Exchange Networks," *American Sociological Review* 43, no. 5 (1978): 721–739; K. S. Cook, R. M. Emerson, M. R. Gillmore, and T. Yamagishi, "The Distribution of Power in Exchange Networks: Theory and Experimental Results," *American Journal of Sociology* 89, no. 2 (1983): 275–305; T. Yamagishi, M. R. Gillmore, and K. S. Cook, "Network Connections and the Distribution of Power in Exchange Networks," *American Journal of Sociology* 93, no. 4 (1988): 833–851; D. Krackhardt, "Assessing the Political Landscape: Structure, Cognition, and Power in Organizations," *Administrative Science Quarterly* 35 (1990): 342–369; and D. Brass and M. Burkhardt, "Potential Power and Power Use: An Investigation of Structure and Behavior," *Academy of Management Journal* 36, no. 3 (1993): 441–470.

8. S. Nadel, *The Theory of Social Structure* (New York: Free Press, 1957); J. Mitchell, "The Concept and Use of Social Networks," in *Social Networks in Urban Situations*, ed. J. Mitchell (Manchester, UK: Manchester University Press, 1969) 1–50; H. White, *An Anatomy of Kinship* (Englewood Cliffs, NJ: Prentice-Hall, 1963); and J. Boyd, "The Algebra of Group Kinship," *Journal of Mathematical Psychology* 6 (1969): 139–167.

9. E. Rogers, *Diffusion of Innovations*, 4th ed. (New York: Free Press, 1995); and T. Valente, *Network Models of the Diffusion of Innovations* (Cresskill, NJ: Hampton Press, 1995).

10. A. Bavelas, "Communication Patterns in Task-Oriented Groups," *Journal of Acoustical Society of America* 22 (1950): 725–730; and M. Shaw, "Communication Networks," in *Advances in Experimental Social Psychology*, ed. L. Berkowitz (New York: Academic Press, 1964): 111–147.

Chapter 1

1. D. Krackhardt, "Cognitive Social Structures," *Social Networks* 9 (1987): 109–134; D. Krackhardt, "Assessing the Political Landscape: Structure, Cognition, and Power in Organizations," *Administrative Science Quarterly* 35 (1990): 342–369;

T. Casciaro, "Seeing Things Clearly: Social Structure, Personality and Accuracy in Social Network Perception," *Social Networks* 20 (1998): 331–351; and D. Krackhardt and J. Hanson, "Informal Networks: The Company Behind the Chart," *Harvard Business Review* 71 (1993): 104–111.

2. E. Wenger, *Communities of Practice* (Oxford, UK: Oxford University Press, 1998); E. Wenger and W. Snyder, "Communities of Practice: The Organizational Frontier," *Harvard Business Review* 137 (2000): 139–145.

3. M. T. Hansen, "The Search-Transfer Problem: The Role of Weak Ties in Sharing Knowledge Across Organization Subunits," *Administrative Science Quarterly* 44 (1999): 82–111; and M. Hansen, J. Podolny, and J. Pfeffer, "So Many Ties, So Little Time: A Task Contingency Perspective on Corporate Social Capital in Organizations," in *Research in the Sociology of Organizations*, vol. 18, eds. S. M. Gabbay and R. Leenders (Oxford: Elsevier, 2001).

4. A. Bavelas, "Communication Patterns in Task-Oriented Groups," *Journal of Accoustical Society of America* 22 (1950): 725–730; and M. Shaw, "Communication Networks," in *Advances in Experimental Social Psychology*, ed. L. Berkowitz (New York: Academic Press, 1964): 111–147.

5. J. Cummings and R. Cross, "Structural Properties of Work Groups and their Consequences for Performance," *Social Networks* 25(3), (2003): 197–210.

6. R. Cross, T. Davenport, and S. Cantrell, "Rising Above the Crowd: How High Performing Knowledge Workers Differentiate Themselves," Accenture Institute for Strategic Change Working Paper (2003).

7. R. Burt, *Structural Holes* (Cambridge, MA: Harvard University Press, 1992); R. Burt, R. Hogarth, and C. Michaud, "The Social Capital of French and American Managers," *Organization Science* 11, no. 2 (2000): 123–147; and M. Gargiulo and M. Benassi, "Trapped in Your Own Net? Network Cohesion, Structural Holes, and the Adaptation of Social Capital," *Organization Science* 11, no. 2 (2000): 183–196.

8. A. Linden, R. Ball, A. Waldir, and K. Haley, "Gartner's Survey on Managing Information" (Note Number: COM-15-0871. Gartner, Inc., 2002).

9. T. Allen, *Managing the Flow of Technology* (Cambridge, MA: MIT Press, 1977); H. Mintzberg, *The Nature of Managerial Work* (New York: Harper Row, 1973); P. Monge and N. Contractor, "Emergence of Communication Networks," in *Handbook of Organizational Communication*, 2d ed., eds. F. Jablin and L. Putnam (Thousand Oaks, CA: Sage, 2000); E. Rogers, *Diffusion of Innovations*, 4th ed. (New York: Free Press, 1995); J. S. Brown and P. Duguid, "Organizational Learning and Communities-of-Practice: Toward a Unified View of Working, Learning and Innovation," *Organization Science* 2, no. 1 (1991): 40–57; and J. Lave and E. Wenger, *Situated Learning: Legitimate Peripheral Participation* (Cambridge, UK: Cambridge University Press, 1991).

10. R. Cross and L. Baird, "Technology Is Not Enough: Improving Performance by Building Organizational Memory," *Sloan Management Review* 41, no. 3 (2000): 41–54.

11. S. Wasserman and K. Faust, *Social Network Analysis: Methods and Applications* (Cambridge, UK: Cambridge University Press, 1994).

12. S. P. Borgatti, M. G. Everett, and L. C. Freeman, *Ucinet for Windows: Software for Social Network Analysis* (Harvard, MA: Analytic Technologies, 2002).

Chapter 2

1. We have used a variety of analytical routines to detect subgroups. The techniques include clique analysis, n-cliques, n-clans, k-plexes, and lambda sets. For further details see S. Wasserman and K. Faust, *Social Network Analysis: Methods and Applications* (Cambridge, UK: Cambridge University Press, 1994). These algorithms can be found in network packages such as UCINET. See S. P. Borgatti, M. G. Everett, and L. C. Freeman, *Ucinet for Windows: Software for Social Network Analysis* (Harvard, MA: Analytic Technologies, 2002).

2. According to a recent study by McKinsey and Lehman Brothers, on the average it takes fourteen years and an estimated $800 million to develop a successful drug. See R. Leheny, "The Fruits of Genomics: Drug Pipelines Face Indigestion Until the New Biology Ripens" (McKinsey Lehman Brothers report, 2001); see also R. Edmunds III, P. Ma, and C. Tanio, "Splicing a Cost Squeeze into the Genomics Revolution," *McKinsey Quarterly* 2 (2000): 71–82.

Chapter 3

1. S. Borgatti and R. Cross, "A Social Network View of Organizational Learning: Relational and Structural Dimensions of 'Know Who,'" *Management Science* 49 (2003): 432–445.

2. Ibid.

Chapter 4

1. Our colleague Steve Borgatti is also doing similar work with social network methods.

2. Performance, in each case, is the annual human-resource rating of each person. In the three organizations, this was a composite figure based on aggregating project evaluations and some objective data throughout the year. The ratings are not entirely consistent in that each organization might be concerned with different subdimensions of performance in the annual evaluation. However, they are consistent in wording and scale in that each is a general appraisal of a person's performance. The evaluations are also clearly separate from the person's perception of his or her own performance.

Chapter 5

1. M. Granovetter, "The Strength of Weak Ties," *American Journal of Sociology* 81 (1973): 1287–1303; M. Granovetter, *Getting a Job: A Study in Contacts and Careers*, 2d ed. (Chicago: University of Chicago Press, 1994); N. Lin, W. Ensel, and J. Vaughn, "Social Resources and Strength of Ties: Structural Factors in Occupational Status Attainment," *American Sociological Review* 46 (1981): 393–405; and N. Lin, "Social Resources and Instrumental Action," in *Social Structure and Network Analysis*, eds. P. Marsden and N. Lin (Beverly Hills, CA: Sage, 1982): 131–145.

2. R. Burt, *Structural Holes* (Cambridge, MA: Harvard University Press, 1992); R. Burt, R. Hogarth, and C. Michaud, "The Social Capital of French and American Managers," *Organization Science* 11, no. 2 (2000): 123–147; and M. Gargiulo and M. Benassi, "Trapped in Your Own Net? Network Cohesion, Structural Holes, and the Adaptation of Social Capital," *Organization Science* 11, no. 2 (2000): 183–196.

3. A. Mehra, M. Kilduff, and D. Brass, "The Social Networks of High and Low Self-monitors: Implications for Workplace Performance," *Administrative Science Quarterly* 46 (2001):121–146; and R. Burt, J. Jannotta, and J. Mahoney, "Personality Correlates of Structural Holes," *Social Networks* 20 (1998): 63–87.

4. P. Lazersfeld and R. Merton, "Friendship as a Social Process," in *Freedom and Control in Modern Society*, ed. M. Berger (New York: Octagon, 1964).

5. Here we bypass purely structural properties of networks via the well-established structural hole measure (R. Burt, *Structural Holes*, op. cit.) because this metric provides little clue as to what one should do differently. We also do not focus here on communication media, although understanding our biases in relying on face-to-face interaction, telephone calls, e-mail, and instant messaging can sometimes show executives how their use of various media constrains (or enhances) their ability to learn from others.

Chapter 6

1. G. Stasser, "Discovery of Hidden Profiles by Decision-Making Groups: Solving a Problem Versus Making a Judgement," *Journal of Personality and Social Psychology* 63, no. 3 (1992): 426–434; and G. Stasser, "Expert Roles and Information Exchange During Discussion: The Importance of Knowing Who Knows What," *Journal of Experimental Social Psychology* 31 (1995): 244–265.

2. W. Baker, *Achieving Success Through Social Capital: Tapping the Hidden Resources in Your Personal and Business Networks* (San Francisco: Jossey Bass, 2000); and D. Cohen and L. Prusak, *In Good Company* (Cambridge, MA: Harvard Business School Press, 2001).

3. L. Abrams, R. Cross, E. Lesser, and D. Levin, "Nurturing Trust in Knowledge Intensive Work," *The Academy of Management Executives* (in press).

4. Ibid.

5. J. K. Butler Jr., "Toward Understanding and Measuring Conditions of Trust: Evolution of a Conditions of Trust Inventory," *Journal of Management* 17 (1991): 643–663.

6. T. Simmons, "Behavioral Integrity: The Perceived Alignment Between Manager's Words and Deeds as a Research Focus," *Organization Science* 13 (2002): 18–35; and E. Whitener, S. Brodt, A. Korsgaard, and J. Werner, "Managers as Initiators of Trust: An Exchange Relationship Framework for Understanding Managerial Trustworthy Behavior," *Academy of Management Review* 23 (1998): 513–530.

7. Although frequent communication (having a strong tie) is a powerful trust builder, it can also decrease learning over time, because people with whom you have strong ties often know the same things that you do. In contrast, people with whom you have weak ties are good at providing novel information. See M. Granovetter, "The Strength of Weak Ties," *American Journal of Sociology* 81 (1973): 1287–1303. Weak ties also take less effort to sustain over time. See M. T. Hansen, "The Search-Transfer Problem: The Role of Weak Ties in Sharing Knowledge Across Organization Subunits," *Administrative Science Quarterly* 44 (1999): 82–111. Interestingly, one recent study found that the most useful knowledge of all comes from trusted weak ties—people you do not know very well but whom you trust to be benevolent and competent. See D. Levin and R. Cross, "The Strength of Weak Ties You Can Trust,"

Management Science, in press. Consistent with this finding, the other nine trust builders can be applied even when people do not know each other or communicate often.

8. W. Tsai and S. Ghoshal, "Social Capital and Value Creation: The Role of Intrafirm Networks," *Academy of Management Journal* 41, no. 4 (1998): 464–476; N. S. Argyres, "The Impact of Information Technology on Coordination: Evidence from the B-2 'Stealth' Bomber," *Organization Science* 10 (1999): 162–180; D. Dougherty, "Interpretive Barriers to Successful Product Innovation in Large Firms," *Organization Science* 3 (1992): 179–202; and D. Levin, "Transferring Knowledge Within the Organization in the R&D Arena" (Ph.D. diss., Northwestern University, 1999).

9. D. Katz and R. Kahn, *The Social Psychology of Organizations*, 2d ed. (New York: Wiley, 1978); S. Barley, "Technology as an Occasion for Structuring: Evidence from Observations of CT Scanners and the Social Order of Radiology Departments," *Administrative Science Quarterly* 31 (1986): 78–108; S. Barley, "The Alignment of Technology and Structure Through Roles and Networks," *Administrative Science Quarterly* 35 (1990): 61–103; and J. Montgomery, Toward a Role-theoretic Conception of Embeddedness," *American Journal of Sociology* 104 (1998): 92–125.

10. J. Coleman, "Social Capital in the Creation of Human Capital," *American Journal of Sociology* 94 (1988): S95–S120; and F. Fukuyama, *Trust: The Social Virtues and the Creation of Prosperity* (New York: Free Press, 1995).

11. E. Locke and G. Latham, *A Theory of Goal Setting and Task Performance* (Englewood Cliffs, NJ: Prentice-Hall, 1990); F. Luthans and A. Stajkovic, "Reinforce for Performance: The Need to Go Beyond Pay and Even Rewards," *Academy of Management Executive* 13, no. 2 (1999): 49–57; and E. Whitener, S. Brodt, A. Korsgaard, and J. Werner, "Managers as Initiators of Trust: An Exchange Relationship Framework for Understanding Managerial Trustworthy Behavior," *Academy of Management Review* 23 (1998): 513–530.

12. R. Cross, S. Borgatti, and A. Parker, "Making Invisible Work Visible: Using Social Network Analysis to Support Strategic Collaboration," *California Management Review* 44, no. 2 (2002): 25–46.

Chapter 7

1. We are particularly grateful to Bob Thomas for insights in this chapter. Research leading to this work was also partially funded by Accenture's Institute for Strategic Change.

2. We employed a case-based logic in data collection by doing semistructured interviews as per R. Yin, *Case Study Research: Design and Methods*, 2d ed. (Newbury Park, CA: Sage, 1994). Our initial perspective on critical dimensions of organizational context that shape network patterns was informed by a detailed review of the following literatures: a resource-based view of the firm, organizational learning (and particularly ideas regarding path dependence and behavioral aspects of organizational-level learning), organizational design, culture, leadership, and HR practices.

3. H. Mintzberg, *Structure in Fives: Designing Effective Organizations* (Englewood Cliffs, NJ: Prentice Hall, 1993).

4. J. Galbraith, *Competing with Flexible Lateral Organizations* (Reading, MA: Addison-Wesley, 1994).

5. R. Grant, "Prospering in Dynamically-competitive Environments: Organizational Capability as Knowledge Integration," *Organization Science* 7 (1996): 375–387; G. Hamel and C. K. Prahalad, *Competing for the Future: Breakthrough Strategies for Seizing Control of Your Industry and Creating the Markets of Tomorrow* (Cambridge, MA: Harvard Business School Press, 1994); and B. Wernerfelt, "A Resource-Based View of the Firm," *Strategic Management Journal* 5 (1984): 171–181.

6. T. Davenport, *Mission Critical* (Boston: Harvard Business School Press, 2000).

7. D. Nadler, M. Gerstein, and R. Shaw, *Organizational Architecture: Designs for Changing Organizations* (San Francisco: Jossey-Bass, 1992); and T. Davenport, R. Thomas, and S. Cantrell, "The Mysterious Art and Science of Knowledge Worker Performance," *Sloan Management Review* 43, no. 4 (2002): 12–21.

8. T. Allen, *Managing the Flow of Technology* (Cambridge, MA: MIT Press, 1977); and P. Monge and N. Contractor, "Emergence of Communication Networks," in *Handbook of Organizational Communication*, 2d ed., eds. F. Jablin and L. Putnam (Thousand Oaks, CA: Sage, 2000).

9. A great deal of evidence from the social sciences points to the importance of a person's network as an asset critically important to performance and career development. See, for example, J. Coleman, "Social Capital in the Creation of Human Capital," *American Journal of Sociology* 94 (1988): S95–S120; R. Burt, *Structural Holes* (Cambridge, MA: Harvard University Press, 1992); and W. Baker, *Achieving Success Through Social Capital: Tapping the Hidden Resources in Your Personal and Business Networks* (San Francisco: Jossey-Bass, 2000).). Given the extent to which people find information and learn how to do their work from relationships, a personal network is a critical asset that professional development processes must support in organizations.

10. T. Brown and K. Iverson, "The Art of Keeping Management Simple: An Interview with Ken Iverson of Nucor Steel," *Harvard Management Update* (May 1988): pp. 2–5.

11. P. Scott-Morgan, *The Unwritten Rules of the Game* (New York: McGraw-Hill, 1994).

Chapter 8

1. This chapter was developed from our own experience and interviews with many people who have been thinking about these issues for some time. We are very grateful for the time of Paul Adler, Dan Brass, Wayne Baker, Noshir Contractor, Kathleen Carley, Malcolm Gladwell, Ranjay Gulati, Monica Higgins, Herminia Ibarra, David Krackhardt, Valdis Krebs, Nitin Nohria, Larry Prusak, and Barry Wellman. These discussions were a high point of this project.

2. B. Gomes-Casseres, "Group Versus Group: How Alliance Networks Compete," *Harvard Business Review* 72 (1994): 62–74; B. Gomes-Casseres, *The Alliance Revolution: The New Shape of Business Rivalry* (Cambridge, MA: Harvard University Press, 1996); J. Moore, *Death of Competition: Leadership and Strategy in the Age of Business Ecosystems* (New York: Harper Business, 1996); and J. Bamford, M. Robinson, and B. Gomes-Casseres, *Mastering Alliance Strategy: A Comprehensive Guide to Design, Management, and Organization* (San Francisco: Jossey-Bass, 2002).

3. R. Gulati, S. Huffman, and G. Neilson, "The Barista Principle: Starbucks and the Rise of Relational Capital," *Strategy and Business* 28 (2002); and R. Gulati,

"Network Location and Learning: The Influence of Network Resources and Firm Capabilities on Alliance Formation," *Strategic Management Journal* 20, no. 5 (1999): 397–420.

4. M. Castells, *The Rise of the Network Society*, 2d ed. (Malden, MA: Blackwell Publishers, 2000): 216–302.

5. For some notable exceptions, see M. Burkhardt and D. Brass, "Changing Patterns or Patterns of Change: The Effects of a Change in Technology on Social Network Structure and Power," *Administrative Science Quarterly* 35, no. 1 (1990): 104–127; M. Burkhardt, "Social Interaction Effects following a Technological Change: A Longitudinal Investigation," *Academy of Management Journal* 37, no. 4 (1994): 869–898; and G. Ahuja, "Collaboration Networks, Structural Holes, and Innovation: A Longitudinal Study," *Administrative Science Quarterly* 45, no. 3 (2000): 425–455.

6. H. Ibarra, "Homophily and Differential Returns: Sex Differences in Network Structure and Access in an Advertising Firm," *Administrative Science Quarterly* 37 (1992): 471–501; H. Ibarra and S. Andrews, "Power, Social Influence, and Sense Making: Effects of Network Centrality and Proximity on Employee Perceptions," *Administrative Science Quarterly* 38 (1993): 277–303; H. Ibarra, "Race, Opportunity, and Diversity of Social Circles in Managerial Networks," *Academy of Management Journal* 38, no. 3 (1995): 673–703; D. Krackhardt and L. Porter, "When Friends Leave: A Structural Analysis of the Relationship Between Turnover and Stayers' Attitudes," *Administrative Science Quarterly* 30 (1985): 242–261; D. Krackhardt, "The Strength of Strong Ties: The Importance of Philos in Organizations," in *Networks and Organizations: Structures, Form and Action*, eds. N. Nohria and R. Eccles (Boston: Harvard Business School Press, 1992), 216–239; D. Krackhardt and J. Hanson, "Informal Networks: The Company Behind the Chart," *Harvard Business Review* 71, (1993): 104–111; and A. Zaheer, B. McEvily, and V. Perrone, "Does Trust Matter? Exploring the Effects of Interorganizational and Interpersonal Trust on Performance," *Organization Science* 9, no. 2 (1998): 141–159.

7. G. Labianca, D. J. Brass, and B. L. Gray, "Social Networks and Perceptions of Intergroup Conflict: The Role of Negative Relationships and Third Parties," *Academy of Management Journal* 41 (1998): 55–67.

Appendix A

1. If people used the same means of referring to the people they listed (or employed a unique identifier such as a phone number for each person), it would be possible to generate full network diagrams. Such an approach would be different from what we describe here because it would rely on recollection rather than asking people to rate lists of names given to them. Still, this seems to be a fruitful avenue because it would save time in the survey process.

2. We typically rely on Freeman's three measures of centrality; see L. Freeman, "Centrality in Social Networks: Conceptual Clarification," *Social Networks* 1 (1979): 215–239. Other measures that we have found useful include structural equivalence, structural holes, and several of the subgroup measures including cliques, n-cliques, and n-clans. For a good discussion of network measures, see J. Scott, *Social Network Analysis*, 2d ed. (Thousand Oaks, CA: Sage, 2000); and A. Degenne and M. Forsé, *Introducing Social Networks* (London: Sage, 1999).

Bibliography

Abrams, L., R. Cross, E. Lesser, and D. Levin. "Nurturing Trust in Knowledge Intensive Work." *The Academy of Management Executives* (in press).

Ahuja, G. "Collaboration Networks, Structural Holes, and Innovation: A Longitudinal Study." *Administrative Science Quarterly* 45, no. 3 (2000): 425–455.

Allen, T. *Managing the Flow of Technology.* Cambridge, MA: MIT Press, 1977.

Argyres, N. S. "The Impact of Information Technology on Coordination: Evidence from the B-2 'Stealth' Bomber." *Organization Science* 10 (1999): 162–180.

Baker, W. *Achieving Success Through Social Capital: Tapping the Hidden Resources in Your Personal and Business Networks.* San Francisco: Jossey-Bass, 2000.

Baker, W., R. Cross, and M. Wooten. "Positive Organizational Network Analysis and Energizing Relationships." In *Positive Organizational Scholarship*, edited by K. Cameron, J. Dutton, and R. Quinn. San Francisco: Berrett-Koehler Publishers, 2003.

Bamford, J., M. Robinson, and B. Gomes-Casseres. *Mastering Alliance Strategy: A Comprehensive Guide to Design, Management, and Organization.* San Francisco: Jossey-Bass, 2002.

Barley, S. "Technology as an Occasion for Structuring: Evidence from Observations of CT Scanners and the Social Order of Radiology Departments." *Administrative Science Quarterly* 31 (1986): 78–108.

Barley, S. "The Alignment of Technology and Structure Through Roles and Networks." *Administrative Science Quarterly* 35 (1990): 61–103.

Bavelas, A. "Communication Patterns in Task-Oriented Groups." *Journal of Acoustical Society of America* 22 (1950): 725–730.

Blau, P. *Exchange and Power in Social Life.* New York: Wiley, 1964.

Borgatti, S., M. G. Everett, and L. C. Freeman. *UCINET for Windows: Software for Social Network Analysis.* Harvard, MA: Analytic Technologies, 2002.

Borgatti, S., and R. Cross. "A Social Network View of Organizational Learning: Relational and Structural Dimensions of 'Know Who.'" *Management Science* 49 (2003): 432–445.

Boyd, J. "The Algebra of Group Kinship." *Journal of Mathematical Psychology* 6 (1969): 139–167.

Brass, D., and M. Burkhardt. "Potential Power and Power Use: An Investigation of Structure and Behavior." *Academy of Management Journal* 36, no. 3 (1993): 441–470.

Brown, J. S., and P. Duguid. "Organizational Learning and Communities-of-Practice: Toward a Unified View of Working, Learning and Innovation." *Organization Science* 2, no. 1 (1991): 40–57.

Brown, T., and K. Iverson. "The Art of Keeping Management Simple: An Interview with Ken Iverson of Nucor Steel." *Harvard Management Update* (May 1988).

Burkhardt, M. "Social Interaction Effects following a Technological Change: A Longitudinal Investigation." *Academy of Management Journal* 37, no. 4 (1994): 869–898.

Burkhardt, M., and D. Brass. "Changing Patterns or Patterns of Change: The Effects of a Change in Technology on Social Network Structure and Power." *Administrative Science Quarterly* 35, no. 1 (1990): 104–127.

Burt, R. *Structural Holes.* Cambridge, MA: Harvard University Press, 1992.

Burt, R., J. Jannotta, and J. Mahoney. "Personality Correlates of Structural Holes." *Social Networks* 20 (1998): 63–87.

Burt, R., R. Hogarth, and C. Michaud. "The Social Capital of French and American Managers." *Organization Science* 11, no. 2 (2000): 123–147.

Butler Jr., J. K. "Toward Understanding and Measuring Conditions of Trust: Evolution of a Conditions of Trust Inventory." *Journal of Management* 17 (1991): 643–663.

Casciaro, T. "Seeing Things Clearly: Social Structure, Personality and Accuracy in Social Network Perception." *Social Networks* 20 (1998): 331–351.

Castells, M. *The Rise of the Network Society.* 2d ed. Malden, MA: Blackwell Publishers, 2000.

Cohen, D., and L. Prusak. *In Good Company.* Cambridge, MA: Harvard Business School Press, 2001.

Coleman, J. "Social Capital in the Creation of Human Capital." *American Journal of Sociology* 94 (1988): S95–S120.

Cook, K. S., and R. M. Emerson. "Power, Equity and Commitment in Exchange Networks." *American Sociological Review* 43, no. 5 (1978): 721–739.

Cook, K. S., R. M. Emerson, M. R. Gillmore, and T. Yamagishi. "The Distribution of Power in Exchange Networks: Theory and Experimental Results." *American Journal of Sociology* 89, no. 2 (1983): 275–305.

Cross, R., and L. Baird. "Technology Is Not Enough: Improving Performance by Building Organizational Memory." *Sloan Management Review* 41, no. 3 (2000): 41–54.

Cross, R., and L. Prusak. "The People Who Make Organizations Go—or Stop." *Harvard Business Review* 80, no. 6 (2002): 1–22.

Cross, R., and L. Prusak. "The Political Economy of Knowledge Markets in Organizations." In *Blackwell Handbook of Organizational Learning and Knowledge Management,* edited by M. Lyle and M. Easterby-Smith. Oxford, UK: Blackwell, 2003.

Cross, R., S. Borgatti, and A. Parker. "Making Invisible Work Visible: Using Social Network Analysis to Support Strategic Collaboration." *California Management Review* 44, no. 2 (2002): 25–46.

Cross, R., T. Davenport, and S. Cantrell. "Rising Above the Crowd: How High Performing Knowledge Workers Differentiate Themselves." Working paper, Accenture Institute for Strategic Change, 2003.

Cross, R., W. Baker, and A. Parker. "What Creates Energy in Organizations?" *Sloan Management Review* 44, no. 4 (2003): 51–56.

Cross, R., A. Parker, L. Prusak, and S. P. Borgatti. "Knowing What We Know: Supporting Knowledge Creation and Sharing in Social Networks." *Organizational Dynamics* 30, no. 2 (2001): 100–120.

Cummings, J., and R. Cross. "Structural Properties of Work Groups and Their Consequences for Performance." *Social Networks* 25, no. 3 (2003): 197–210.

Davenport, T. *Mission Critical*. Boston: Harvard Business School Press, 2000.

Davenport, T., R. Thomas, and S. Cantrell. "The Mysterious Art and Science of Knowledge Worker Performance." *Sloan Management Review* 43, no. 4 (2002).

Degenne, A., and M. Forsé. *Introducing Social Networks*. London: Sage, 1999.

Dougherty, D. "Interpretive Barriers to Successful Product Innovation in Large Firms." *Organization Science* 3 (1992): 179–202.

Edmunds III, R., P. Ma, and C. Tanio. "Splicing a Cost Squeeze into the Genomics Revolution." *McKinsey Quarterly* 2 (2000).

Emerson, R. M. "Power-Dependence Relations." *American Sociological Review* 27 (1962): 31–41.

Freeman, L. "Centrality in Social Networks: Conceptual Clarification." *Social Networks* 1 (1979): 215–239.

Fukuyama, F. *Trust: The Social Virtues and the Creation of Prosperity*. New York: Free Press, 1995.

Gabbay, S., and R. Leenders. *Social Capital in Organizations*. Stamford, CT: JAI Press, 2001.

Galbraith, J. *Competing with Flexible Lateral Organizations*. Reading, MA: Addison-Wesley, 1994.

Galbraith, J. *Designing Organizations: An Executive Briefing on Strategy, Structure, and Process*. San Francisco: Jossey-Bass, 1995.

Gargiulo, M., and M. Benassi. "Trapped in Your Own Net? Network Cohesion, Structural Holes, and the Adaptation of Social Capital." *Organization Science* 11, no. 2 (2000): 183–196.

Gomes-Casseres, B. "Group Versus Group: How Alliance Networks Compete." *Harvard Business Review* 72 (1994): 62–74.

Gomes-Casseres, B. *The Alliance Revolution: The New Shape of Business Rivalry*. Cambridge, MA: Harvard University Press, 1996.

Granovetter, M. "The Strength of Weak Ties." *American Journal of Sociology* 81 (1973): 1287–1303.

Granovetter, M. *Getting a Job: A Study in Contacts and Careers*. 2d ed. Chicago: University of Chicago Press, 1994.

Grant, R. "Prospering in Dynamically-competitive Environments: Organizational Capability as Knowledge Integration." *Organization Science* 7 (1996): 375–387.

Gulati, R. "Social Structure and Alliance Formation Patterns: A Longitudinal Analysis." *Administrative Science Quarterly* 40 (1995): 619–652.

Gulati, R. "Network Location and Learning: The Influence of Network Resources and Firm Capabilities on Alliance Formation." *Strategic Management Journal* 20, no. 5 (1999): 397–420.

Gulati, R. "Where Do Interorganizational Networks Come From?" *American Journal of Sociology* 104, no. 5 (1999): 1439–1493.

Gulati, R., S. Huffman, and G. Neilson. "The Barista Principal: Starbucks and the Rise of Relational Capital." *Strategy and Business* 28 (2002).

Hamel, G., and C. K. Prahalad. *Competing for the Future: Breakthrough Strategies for Seizing Control of Your Industry and Creating the Markets of Tomorrow*. Cambridge, MA: Harvard Business School Press, 1994.

Handy, C. *The Age of Paradox*. Boston: Harvard Business School Press, 1994.

Hansen, M. T. "The Search-Transfer Problem: The Role of Weak Ties in Sharing Knowledge Across Organization Subunits." *Administrative Science Quarterly* 44 (1999): 82–111.

Hansen, M., J. Podolny, and J. Pfeffer. "So Many Ties, So Little Time: A Task Contingency Perspective on Corporate Social Capital in Organizations." In *Research in the Sociology of Organizations*, vol. 18, edited by S. M. Gabbay and R. Leenders. Oxford: Elsevier, 2001.

Heckscher, C. "Defining the Post-bureaucratic Type." In *The Post-bureaucratic Organization: New Perspectives on Organizational Change*, edited by C. Heckscher and A. Donnellon. Thousand Oaks, CA: Sage, 1994.

Ibarra, H. "Homophily and Differential Returns: Sex Differences in Network Structure and Access in an Advertising Firm." *Administrative Science Quarterly* 36 (1992): 471–501.

Ibarra, H. "Race, Opportunity, and Diversity of Social Circles in Managerial Networks." *Academy of Management Journal* 38, no. 3 (1995): 673–703.

Ibarra, H., and S. Andrews. "Power, Social Influence, and Sense Making: Effects of Network Centrality and Proximity on Employee Perceptions." *Administrative Science Quarterly* 38 (1993): 277–303.

Katz, D., and R. Kahn. *The Social Psychology of Organizations*. 2d ed. New York: Wiley, 1978.

Krackhardt, D. "Assessing the Political Landscape: Structure, Cognition, and Power in Organizations." *Administrative Science Quarterly* 35 (1990): 342–369.

Krackhardt, D. "Cognitive Social Structures." *Social Networks* 9 (1987): 109–134.

Krackhardt, D. "The Strength of Strong Ties: The Importance of Philos in Organizations." In *Networks and Organizations: Structures, Form and Action*, edited by N. Nohria and R. Eccles, 216–239. Boston: Harvard Business School Press, 1992.

Krackhardt, D., and J. Hanson. "Informal Networks: The Company Behind the Chart." *Harvard Business Review* 71 (1993): 104–111.

Krackhardt, D., and L. Porter. "When Friends Leave: A Structural Analysis of the Relationship Between Turnover and Stayers' Attitudes." *Administrative Science Quarterly* 30 (1985): 242–261.

Labianca, G., D. J. Brass, and B. L. Gray. "Social Networks and Perceptions of Intergroup Conflict: The Role of Negative Relationships and Third Parties." *Academy of Management Journal* 41 (1998): 55–67.

Lave, J., and E. Wenger. *Situated Learning: Legitimate Peripheral Participation*. Cambridge, UK: Cambridge University Press, 1991.

Lazersfeld, P., and R. Merton. "Friendship as a Social Process." In *Freedom and Control in Modern Society*, edited by M. Berger. New York: Octagon, 1964.

Leenders, R., and S. Gabbay. *Corporate Social Capital and Liability*. New York: Kluwer, 1999.

Leheny, R. "The Fruits of Genomics: Drug Pipelines Face Indigestion Until the New Biology Ripens." McKinsey Lehman Brothers report, 2001.

Levin, D. "Transferring Knowledge Within the Organization in the R&D Arena." Ph.D. diss., Northwestern University, 1999.

Levin, D., and R. Cross, "The Strength of Weak Ties You Can Trust: The Mediating Role of Trust in Effective Knowledge Transfer." *Management Science*, in press.

Lin, N. "Social Resources and Instrumental Action." In *Social Structure and Network Analysis*, edited by P. Marsden and N. Lin, 131–145. Beverly Hills, CA: Sage, 1982.

Lin, N., K. S. Cook, and R. S. Burt. *Social Capital: Theory and Research*. New York: Aldine de Gruyter, 2001.

Lin, N., W. Ensel, and J. Vaughn. "Social Resources and Strength of Ties: Structural Factors in Occupational Status Attainment." *American Sociological Review* 46 (1981): 393–405.

Linden, A., R. Ball, A. Waldir, and K. Haley. "Gartner's Survey on Managing Information." Note Number: COM-15-0871. Gartner, Inc., 2002.

Locke, E., and G. Latham. *A Theory of Goal Setting and Task Performance*. Englewood Cliffs, NJ: Prentice-Hall, 1990.

Luthans, F., and A. Stajkovic. "Reinforce for Performance: The Need to Go Beyond Pay and Even Rewards." *Academy of Management Executives* 13, no. 2 (1999): 49–57.

Mehra, A., M. Kilduff, and D. Brass. "The Social Networks of High and Low Self-monitors: Implications for Workplace Performance." *Administrative Science Quarterly* 46 (2001): 121–146.

Miles, R., and C. Snow. *Fit, Failure, and the Hall of Fame: How Companies Succeed or Fail*. New York: Free Press, 1994.

Miles, R., and C. Snow. "Network Organizations: New Concepts for New Forms." *California Management Review* 28 (1986): 62–73.

Miles, R., and C. Snow. "The New Network Firm: A Spherical Structure Built on a Human Investment Policy." *Organizational Dynamics* 23, no. 4 (1995): 5–18.

Mintzberg, H. *Structure in Fives: Designing Effective Organizations*. Englewood Cliffs, NJ: Prentice Hall, 1993.

Mintzberg, H. *The Nature of Managerial Work*. New York: Harper Row, 1973.

Mitchell, J. "The Concept and Use of Social Networks." In *Social Networks in Urban Situations*, edited by J. Mitchell, 1–50. Manchester, UK: Manchester University Press, 1969.

Monge, P., and N. Contractor. "Emergence of Communication Networks." In *Handbook of Organizational Communication*, 2d ed., edited by F. Jablin and L. Putnam. Thousand Oaks, CA: Sage, 2000.

Monge, P., and N. Contractor. *Theories of Communication Networks*. New York: Oxford University Press, 2003.

Montgomery, J. "Toward a Role-theoretic Conception of Embeddedness." *American Journal of Sociology* 104 (1998): 92–125.

Moore, J. *Death of Competition: Leadership and Strategy in the Age of Business Ecosystems*. New York: Harper Business, 1996.

Moreno, J. *Who Shall Survive?* Washington, DC: Nervous and Mental Disease Publishing Company, 1934.

Nadel, S. *The Theory of Social Structure.* New York: Free Press, 1957.

Nadler, D., M. Gerstein, and R. Shaw. *Organizational Architecture: Designs for Changing Organizations.* San Francisco: Jossey-Bass, 1992.

New York Times, 3 April 1933: L17.

Rogers, E. *Diffusion of Innovations.* 4th ed. New York: Free Press, 1995.

Scott, J. *Social Network Analysis.* 2d ed. Thousand Oaks, CA: Sage Publications, 2000.

Scott-Morgan, P. *The Unwritten Rules of the Game.* New York: McGraw-Hill, 1994.

Shaw, M. "Communication Networks." In *Advances in Experimental Social Psychology,* edited by L. Berkowitz, 111–147. New York: Academic Press, 1964.

Simmons, T. "Behavioral Integrity: The Perceived Alignment Between Manager's Words and Deeds as a Research Focus." *Organization Science* 13 (2002): 18–35.

Stasser, G. "Discovery of Hidden Profiles by Decision-Making Groups: Solving a Problem Versus Making a Judgement." *Journal of Personality and Social Psychology* 63, no. 3 (1992): 426–434.

Stasser, G. "Expert Roles and Information Exchange During Discussion: The Importance of Knowing Who Knows What." *Journal of Experimental Social Psychology* 31 (1995): 244–265.

Tsai, W., and S. Ghoshal. "Social Capital and Value Creation: The Role of Intrafirm Networks." *Academy of Management Journal* 41, no. 4 (1998): 464–476.

Uzzi, B. "Social Structure and Competition in Interfirm Networks: The Paradox of Embeddedness." *Administrative Science Quarterly* 42 (1997): 35–67.

Uzzi, B. "The Sources and Consequences of Embeddedness for the Economic Performance of Organizations: The Network Effect." *American Sociological Review* 61 (1996): 674–698.

Valente, T. *Network Models of the Diffusion of Innovations.* Cresskill, NJ: Hampton Press, 1995.

Wasserman, S., and K. Faust. *Social Network Analysis: Methods and Applications.* Cambridge, UK: Cambridge University Press, 1994.

Wellman, B. "Different Strokes from Different Folks: Community Ties and Social Support." *American Journal of Sociology* 96, no. 3 (1990): 558–588.

Wellman, B. "The Community Question: The Intimate Networks of East Yorkers." *American Journal of Sociology* 84, no. 5 (1979): 1201–1231.

Wellman, B., J. Salaff, D. Dimitrova, L. Garton, M. Gulia, and C. Haythornthwaite. "Computer Networks as Social Networks: Collaborative Work, Telework, and Virtual Community." *Annual Review of Sociology* 22 (1996): 213–238.

Wenger, E. *Communities of Practice.* Oxford, UK: Oxford University Press, 1998.

Wenger, E., and W. Snyder. "Communities of Practice: The Organizational Frontier." *Harvard Business Review* 137 (2000): 139–145.

Wernerfelt, B. "A Resource Based View of the Firm." *Strategic Management Journal* 5 (1984): 171–181.

White, H. *An Anatomy of Kinship.* Englewood Cliffs, NJ: Prentice-Hall, 1963.

Whitener, E., S. Brodt, A. Korsgaard, and J. Werner. "Managers as Initiators of Trust: An Exchange Relationship Framework for Understanding Managerial Trustworthy Behavior." *Academy of Management Review* 23 (1998): 513–530.

Yamagishi, T., M. R. Gillmore, and K. S. Cook. "Network Connections and the Distribution of Power in Exchange Networks." *American Journal of Sociology* 93, no. 4 (1988): 833–851.

Yin, R. *Case Study Research: Design and Methods.* 2d ed. Newbury Park, CA: Sage, 1994.

Zaheer, A., B. McEvily, and V. Perrone. "Does Trust Matter? Exploring the Effects of Interorganizational and Interpersonal Trust on Performance." *Organization Science* 9, no. 2 (1998): 141–159.

Index

About the Authors

ROB CROSS is an assistant professor of management at the University of Virginia's McIntire School of Commerce. He also directs the social network research program for IBM's Knowledge and Organizational Performance Forum, where he has worked with a wide range of well-known companies and government agencies in applying network concepts to critical business issues. Rob's work on social networks has been published in such venues as *Harvard Business Review, Sloan Management Review, California Management Review, Organizational Dynamics,* and *Business Horizons.* Rob speaks, consults, and conducts executive education both domestically and internationally.

ANDREW PARKER is a research consultant with the IBM Knowledge and Organizational Performance Forum in Cambridge, Massachusetts. He has conducted research in a wide range of *Fortune* 500 organizations and government agencies. His research has covered top-level executive teams, functional departments, communities of practice, and recently merged companies. This research has helped these organizations develop insight into critical knowledge creation and sharing activities. Andrew has coauthored more than ten articles and one anthology on network analysis. His articles have appeared in *Sloan Management Review, Organizational Dynamics,* and *California Management Review.* He is a doctoral student at Stanford University and holds graduate degrees from Northeastern University and the London School of Economics.